Teaching the

BOOK 1

S.M.A.R.T.S.™

Way

Teaching the S.M.A.R.T..S.™ Way, Book 1
Published by S.M.A.R.T.S. Learning System™
A division of Recreational Education Enterprises, L.L.C.
P.O. Box 7930
Waco, TX 76714-7930
www.smartslearningsystem.com

S.M.A.R.T.S. Learning System™
P.O. Box 7930
Waco, TX 76714-7930

www.smartslearningsystem.com

254-776-6664

ISBN 0-9709634-0-8 (4 Volume Set)
ISBN 0-9709634-1-6 (Volume 1)
ISBN 0-9709634-2-4 (Volume 2)
ISBN 0-9709634-3-2 (Volume 3)
ISBN 0-9709634-4-0 (Volume 4)

Library of Congress Control Number 2001087990

Cover Design: Terry M. Roller. Front Cover Photography: Susan Dunkerley

ALL I REALLY NEED TO KNOW I LEARNED IN KINDERGARTEN
by Robert Fulghum, copyright © 1986, 1988 by Robert L. Fulghum.
Used by permission of Villard Books, a division of Random House, Inc.

S.M.A.R.T.S.™ and S.M.A.R.T.S. Learning System™
are trademarks of Recreational Education Enterprises, L.L.C., Waco, Texas.

Printed in the United States of America
by CORD Communications, 324 Kelly Dr., Waco, TX 76710.

Teaching the

BOOK 1

S.M.A.R.T.S.™

Way

Teaching Strategies That Really Work!

by Lauretta Buchanan

Learning System™

Recreational Education Enterprises, L.L.C.,
P.O. Box 7930, Waco, Texas, 76714-7930

www.smartslearningsystem.com

**Other books and products from
S.M.A.R.T.S. Learning System™ and Lauretta Buchanan:**

Teaching the S.M.A.R.T.S.™ Way, Teaching Strategies that Really Work, Book 2

Book 2 includes these five proven teaching strategies:

Figure It Out™
Stump the Teacher™
Decision Writing™
Skim and Scan™
Make a Choice, Take a Chance™

Watch for S.M.A.R.T.S.™ Shortcuts Booklets. Each booklet is a mini-unit of curriculum content with a test review, sample tests, and suggested student activities. Perfect for introducing content, remediation, testing, clarification, and to use as supplemental materials and for makeup work. These booklets are written for all grade levels and academic subjects including Math, History, Language Arts, Social Studies, Science, and Geography. Watch, too, for the S.M.A.R.T.S.™ Shortcuts series on parenting, communication, self-esteem, motivation, and behavior management.

Also available,
S.M.A.R.T.S.™ T-shirts, caps, and other merchandise,
which work as great motivational rewards for your S.M.A.R.T.S.™ Intelligence Team Scholars.

To book a S.M.A.R.T.S.™
seminar, training session, in-service training, or to purchase other products,
Recreational Education Enterprises
P.O. Box 7930
Waco, Texas 76714-7930

www.smartslearningsystem.com

254-776-6664
Fax: 254-776-3136

Dedication:

*To all the teachers, students, parents, and friends
who have taught me everything I know and
continue to teach me on a daily basis.*

Acknowledgments

Being a first-time author is an enlightening experience for all concerned. (This basically means very few of us actually know what we're doing!) To the following people, I especially say "Thanks." If not for them, I'd still be on Chapter 1, page 2, and those would probably need redoing!

I thank first my beloved husband, who bankrolled this whole project. He also gave love, his moral support, proofed twice, and filed once.

To my business partner and precious friend Elinor Davis, I dedicate this and all the books, because everything I read to her she says, "That's good." I think she's pretty close to a nervous breakdown, but does any- and everything to make things work out. I've noticed lately she laughs a lot and is developing a slight twitch.

I thank "my boys" who have called Mom, incessantly telling me how proud they are; what a success I'm going to be; could I be one soon; and please send money!

I thank Eric Lundquist, who first started me in this business by taking me to a marketing group, telling them I wanted to write strategies for teachers and kids, and that I didn't care that much about the money. He's right. I think he's raising cows, emus, and a bull somewhere in Texas.

I must thank Terry Roller who has made S.M.A.R.T.S.™ look professional from the outset. He pulls everything together and his patience, willingness, and talent are unmatched although his first love is Karaoke! He has been an avid supporter of S.M.A.R.T.S.™ from the beginning.

My buddy, Sandra Bloom was my first editor. We still work together even though she says things to me like, "This is too wordy. You don't need this in here—it doesn't fit." And, "This is okay, Lauretta, but quite honestly, I've heard you better. " Now that's a real friend!

To Martha Hopkins, for whom I'm extremely grateful and who writes cookbooks. She covered my drafts with red ink, is obviously a good editor, and undoubtedly a darned good cook!

I thank Connie Garza. She does my hair, covers the roots, and just generally makes me look and feel better. Naturally, when I look and feel better, I write better because I can work without fearing that people think I'm so consumed with this writing thing that I've just totally let myself go. She's probably the glue that holds everything together.

I thank all the people who have asked questions in my workshops. These folks made me rethink what I've done, consequently I worked even harder so all their questions could be adequately and satisfactorily answered. They make me better than I am.

Above all, I must thank the numerous kids who, through the years, needed my help and made their necessity my "mother of invention." It was for them that this process was begun. I wish each of them continued success.

—Lauretta

Teaching the **BOOK 1**

S.M.A.R.T.S.™

Way

CONTENTS

S.M.A.R.T.S. Learning System™—Teaching Strategies That Really Work

My father-in-law once said to my husband, "When you go to a meeting and bring back one good idea that helps you do a better job, you've just paid for the trip."

Welcome to the S.M.A.R.T.S. Learning System.™ This collection of classroom teaching strategies addresses both academic and behavioral objectives by combining direct instruction and cooperative learning. They are strict, consistent, and they work!

The days of lecturing in front of the class while students follow along in the reading are almost over! The days of pulling kids into the subject matter, making lessons relevant and meaningful, of piquing students' curiosity and natural propensity to learn have arrived. In this fast-paced, high-tech, interactive world of the twenty-first century, active participatory learning is the only way teachers are going to reach and teach today's youngsters. The S.M.A.R.T.S. Learning System™ helps teachers engage their students in just such a way.

I realized a long time ago that although I couldn't *make* kids learn, I could get their attention and get them to behave for short periods of time. But to keep their attention and help them learn, I had to find a way to stop misbehavior and engage kids in the lesson. I had to put positive peer pressure to work in the classroom to enhance learning.

There is a line from an old song that goes, "What's the matter with kids today?" As a teacher, I am sure you've sometimes felt you couldn't control your classroom. Believe me, I've been there. It's not you. It's not a curse. It's kids. It's a by-product of the world we live in. But you *can* control behavior in the classroom by pulling kids into the lesson and making class assignments participatory and fun, instead of worksheets and book work. By unleashing children's natural tendencies to compete and to do well in the eyes of their peers, teachers can achieve levels of both classroom decorum and active learning that many have only dreamed of.

The teaching strategies that comprise the S.M.A.R.T.S. Learning System™ use systems of clues and interactive communication among students to bring classrooms and learning to life. These strategies made a real impact on me *and* my students in the classroom, and when I started doing conferences and workshops, I saw their value in communicating with conference attendees as well. Seminar participants (and students) want to do just that—participate. They don't want to be read to. They don't want lecture any more than our students want it. They want to learn by doing . . . by seeing, hearing, talking, reasoning, experiencing, explaining. They want to use their own words to formulate vivid descriptions and mental images so that the subject at hand means something. By utilizing self-talk and rational thinking, information begins to make sense, knowledge and ideas get shared, and new knowledge and ideas grow. Learning becomes personal. It matters. The whole learning experience is enriched, which in turn enriches lives—yours as well as your students! This is the first in a series of *Teaching the S.M.A.R.T.S.™ Way* books. My goal quite honestly is to help the educational process by encouraging all students to become active learners. Each *Teaching the S.M.A.R.T.S.™ Way* book contains five S.M.A.R.T.S.™ strategies which incorporate either direct instruction, or a combination of direct and truly structured, cooperative learning. Each chapter is one strategy. Each chapter also includes sample lessons and questions with which to practice learning how to use the S.M.A.R.T.S.™ Way to increase student participation in the educational process.

In traveling around the country, the one complaint I hear is that behavior is interfering with learning. Teachers are worn out, burned out, and tired. In defense of the kids, though, too many of them are so behind, frustrated, and lost that their apathy is a defense mechanism. Some are simply waiting until they're old enough to drop out. Parents are overwhelmed. Respect for and acceptance of everyone is slipping away. Pressure on everybody to perform is a continual uphill battle.

We seem to have misplaced our ideals that school is an exciting place where students and teachers want to be, and where learning *how* to learn is as important as learning *what* to learn. Although kids are not alike, the main goal is to prepare each one for life. And to do this we have to teach and model reading processing skills in all content areas on a continuum. Whether we're

checking to see if our students recognize the main idea, the supporting details, or context clues, we can't simply say, "Read Chapter Seven," and expect students to master specific skills. They must be taught reading skills as they read so content makes sense. Students need to practice and receive consistent guidance and be monitored to guarantee improvement. Reading, writing, and math skills should be integrated into every content lesson and activity on a daily basis. These are crucial aspects for a quality education. Sadly they are not often seen as essential. Rather, these ideas appear to have been replaced by competition among schools; state academic scores; teacher evaluations; and achievement based more on a student's testing ability than on the child's actual knowledge. Somewhere along the line we've gotten off track, but we'd better get back on track … and the sooner the better.

I sincerely wish I had all the solutions, that I could twitch my nose and make all the problems go away. But I can't. I can tell you that as a parent and educator, I won't give up and neither should you. Schools aren't just buildings, they're people. It takes all of us working together, praying together, and staying together to get our kids to adulthood. It takes all of us supporting each other for our children to feel supported.

This series of *Teaching the S.M.A.R.T.S.™ Way* books doesn't preach or spout theory. The books are simply a collection of practical, common sense, easy-to-learn-and-use teaching and learning strategies. The strategies can be used with any subject or grade level—even with adults and businesses. S.M.A.R.T.S.™ strategies are fun. I got the idea of making learning fun by watching my students do things on the computer that they couldn't do at their desks. I also realized that successful team sports are based on the same concept of implementing strict, specific instructions followed by structured cooperative team activities. I was watching the players on a pro team with their coach. Each had his own role in the group. The coach planned what they were to do, and when the individual team members supported each other, were responsible and accountable for carrying out those responsibilities and worked as a team, the team usually won. When the team won, so did each player on the team! I figured that if it works for professional sports, it should certainly work in schools, especially if the goal is for each participant to continually improve and become more involved. That's what S.M.A.R.T.S.™ strategies are—techniques which include strict, specific instruction followed by structured, cooperative, team activities within a classroom setting.

S.M.A.R.T.S.™ techniques are tested, validated tactics that have been proven effective in classrooms throughout the country. Although they are strategies, I always refer to them as *games,* for three primary reasons. First, people like games, so they are more easily motivated to become involved. Second, people follow rules when they are playing games. If they develop a habit of consistently following rules, they are more inclined to follow directions and instructions. And, finally, team activities harness the power of positive peer pressure.

S.M.A.R.T.S.™ strategies teach students *how* to learn more than *what* to learn. They help to improve behavior, introduce content, review information, prepare for testing, and remediate when necessary. S.M.A.R.T.S.™ strategies empower students to become active, creative learners who automatically become an integral part of the learning process.

The same questions, answers, and information can be used with multiple S.M.A.R.T.S.™ strategies to save the instructor time and to add variety to every lesson. Teaching and learning should be enjoyable, challenging, stimulating, common-sense, and practical. These are the objectives of the S.M.A.R.T.S.™ strategies. Use them all, but choose one you really like and get used to it before you go to another. Add your own expertise to improve them. Adapt them to your grade level, subject, and objectives. Let me know what you did to improve my work so I can share your expertise with other educators and users. Only when we become a team, use what works for the learner, and continually strive for improvement will we achieve a win-win situation for everyone involved.

This is my hope. This is why I've worked so many years to develop S.M.A.R.T.S.™ and this is why I want to share it. Become each other's best resources. Learn from each other. Give S.M.A.R.T.S.,™ yourselves, your students, and each other a try. Go for it! If we don't win in education, we have a lot to lose. We can't afford to lose one more child.

—*Lauretta*

CHAPTER 1

CONCENTRATION PLUS™

OR

"These Kids Have Attention Spans the Size of a Gnat's"

Life's lessons are sometimes taught in the most unlikely places. I remember going to a race track in Denver, Colorado. Boy, was I excited! Beautiful, sleek, thoroughbred horses. An atmosphere of fevered frenzy. Everybody was absolutely sure the horse they'd selected would be the first to cross the finish line. I was no exception. I read the Tip Sheet and studied the racing form and carefully thought about the horses as their jockeys paraded them before the crowd. I made my picks to win, place, and show, and breathed a satisfied sigh as the horses were positioned at the starting gate.

Apparently, I looked so self-confident that two elderly ladies in the next box wanted my advice. Full of myself, I explained my choices. One of the women wanted to opt for my number two horse to win. "No! No! No!" I exclaimed. "That horse starts off well, but most of the time he's slow to finish. Pick him to place or show, but not to win. I can promise he won't finish first." Taking my advice, they placed their bets as the starting pistol fired. The race began. Horses bunched together amidst a cloud of dust. As I predicted, my number-two horse took the lead but fell back into second place—one length, two. Perfect! I felt brilliant . . . the 5 o'clock news would want my expertise and commentary on a regular basis. Suddenly, it was as if my second-place horse just gave up. I don't know what happened. I don't know if he forgot he was in a race, didn't recognize the finish line, decided to check out the scenery, or what, but about a hundred yards from victory, that horse just stopped. Even with the jockey coaxing, spurring, trying everything he knew to direct him toward the finish line, my number-two horse just gallivanted around the track kicking up his heels, going the wrong direction, doing his thing. He never even finished the race! As I sat there stunned, two lessons became obvious: One— my advice is not always right and two— the only sure thing is that there are no sure things. Getting off-track is more of a sure thing than any bet. This is equally true for our classrooms and for horse races.

At some time in our classes, we've all felt like that jockey. We've done everything we were supposed to do and it didn't matter. We've coaxed, encouraged, tried—but it didn't work—we just couldn't get through. It feels maddening, frustrating, and esteem-robbing, but it happens. We can create the best lesson ever written, but if our students don't stay on track, it makes no difference. Just as a horse must cross the finish line to win, students must get the point of a lesson for it to count. If they can't pay attention, listen, absorb what is being said, and make sense of the information, learning doesn't happen.

James was one of these students. He was the one who shocked me into realizing and recognizing the magnitude of this problem. Just listening to him read aloud, he sounded perfect, but he couldn't remember anything he'd just read. He did not comprehend the content. I remember having him read a four sentence paragraph, and then asking him questions about what he'd read. He had read the words, but he had processed nothing. He connected nothing. He answered nothing. It hit me like a ton of bricks—word attack is meaning-less without comprehension! It doesn't matter how well a person reads if he doesn't know what he just read. When I asked James questions, he had a blank look on his face. I recall asking him to tell me anything he remembered about the paragraph he had just finished reading. Anything. Not dissect the paragraph. Not be analytical or insightful. Just tell me something, *anything at all* about the silly paragraph. He tried. I could see the effort in his face, the strain behind his eyes, the bewilderment as he tried to make the pieces of information come together. He couldn't do it. He couldn't tell me anything about what he had read. In his mind, the words had no meaning, no connection, no relevancy. They were just words.

James forced me to face the fact that many of my kids could read or speak the words, but could not understand those words, or make sense of what the words meant when they were put together. I think James also made me realize that if I were in Chapter 12 but my kids were still in Chapter 10, then it was both absurd and frustrating for me to be in Chapter 12 all alone. I could tell other teachers, "We're in Chapter 12." But the truth was that I was in Chapter 12; "*We*" weren't. A vital half of "we" were behind, frustrated, and lost. "We" wouldn't get to Chapter 12 until "I" helped the other part of "we" master Chapters 10 and 11. Then "we" could all be in Chapter 12 together. I definitely needed to try something different.

Somehow the students must *want* to listen, must consciously *try* to listen, and then must *recognize* what they were listening for when they heard it. The process had to be fun, challenging, and encouraging; but it also had to be one they'd buy into. If I told them we were going to practice listening skills, they would not only be embarrassed, they would simply write-off the whole idea. Some of those kids learned on a first- or second-grade level even though they were in grades seven through twelve. In my head, I kept going over what I'd heard them—every single one of them—say millions of times when they wanted to use the computer: "Mrs. B, may I go play on the computer?"

Even if kids were doing something difficult on the computer, they considered it "play." Obviously the operative word was "play." So what do you play? Games. It hit me that whatever listening-skills solution I concocted would be most effective if the kids perceived it as a game.

Thus it began . . . I thought, wrote, rewrote, tried, retried, changed, and, yes, labored. My first S.M.A.R.T.S. Learning System™ Strategy, Concentration Plus™ was born. It entered the world flawed, needing to be cleaned up, but it was here and ready to grow. Just like me and my kids, it was a work-in-progress. Thankfully, it has progressed. It has grown, been refined, and improved. It's probably not what it will eventually become, but it worked back then and it works even better today.

As a teacher, I used anything I could get my hands on to help my kids learn and to make my job a little easier. I began using Concentration Plus™ on a regular basis at the beginning of each class period. By using my regular lesson content to play the game, we killed several birds with one stone: the kids could practice their listening and focusing skills while I reviewed key points in the lesson. In the first six minutes of class, my students received an overview of the day's lesson while I covered the lesson objectives. I also threw in a few "food for thought" questions and comments for good measure.

Classroom behavior, habits, and attitudes began to improve. My kids would come into the classroom, go to their desks, put their books away, and get out notebook paper and a pen/pencil, ready to "play" our game. There was none of the usual, "Class, please take your seats. Go to your desks now, please. Class, please stop talking.

Okay, everyone get quiet. Stop talking, right now! Okay, stop it. Stop. Stop. Stop. Class, please . . . please, please, please, please, please." These kids would actually come into the classroom in a reasonably orderly fashion, have their supplies with them, get situated, and wait for me to begin. They looked forward to the game and I looked forward to them.

Since then, thousands of teachers, parents, and other educators have learned to play "my" game. I've watched it successfully practiced with students from kindergarten to college. What began as an idea for one student to improve his attention span and reading comprehension has grown to be an opening activity in classrooms across the country. Because parents and teachers are adding their own flair and using S.M.A.R.T.S.™ Concentration Plus™ to meet their children's needs, they are reinforcing the idea that active learning is an extremely powerful educational tool. They are confirming that a simple technique can involve every student in the classroom and yield amazing results. Thanks to James, a teacher challenged herself to come up with something to help one student learn, and affected the lives of many more students as a result. That's the way successful strategies and techniques come into being: one kid, one teacher, one call for help, and somebody doing whatever he or she can to answer that call. I see it happen in every school I visit. It never ceases to amaze me and make me eternally proud to be a teacher.

S.M.A.R.T.S.™ Concentration Plus™

S.M.A.R.T.S.™ Concentration Plus™ is a game that benefits all students, especially those who lack self-control or have a short attention span, poor comprehension, or retention problems. The game helps students learn to focus on objectives while tuning out unwanted distractions. Concentration Plus™ should be practiced daily for at least three minutes at the beginning of each class period. The game not only helps students settle down into a learning mood, but it also improves listening skills by letting students hear information several times for emphasis. Concentration Plus™ can be used with any subject or grade level in order to master content and lesson objectives. It is an excellent tool for parents to use with their children to improve listening skills, recall, and comprehension.

Although I give a detailed description of one way to play Concentration Plus™, teachers may vary the game so that students listen for nouns, pronouns, verbs, or other parts of speech; context clues; information that is sequentially ordered; data to be summarized; general or specific information; cause-effect; or details. To practice listening and keeping track at the same time, the teacher may ask students to count the number of times they hear a word. Students may be asked to identify antonyms and synonyms, compare and contrast particulars, draw conclusions, predict outcomes, and recognize the feelings and emotions of characters. Younger students may listen for letters of the alphabet, phonetic sounds, colors, names, instructions, dates, and numbers. In essence, teachers may instruct students to listen for whatever they choose.

Instructions

1. Students will need paper and a pen/pencil. They should be seated, heads lowered [chin to chest], eyes closed, so they can better concentrate and not watch the reader's mouth. With paper on the desktop and pencil/pen poised, students are to make marks (draw lines) on the paper according to the teacher's instructions.

2. The teacher begins by reading aloud to the students. When he/she comes to the end of a paragraph or sentence, to a comma, period, another form of punctuation, or to a place where a pause is needed, the teacher pauses by taking a breath or hesitating during the reading. The students are to note the pause or hesitation by making a mark/drawing a line on their paper. It is important that students'

eyes are closed since they tend to watch the reader's mouth and wait for it to stop moving before they make a mark on their paper. (When students watch the reader's mouth rather than listen, the strategy's purpose is defeated. The purpose is for students to learn to listen; and then, to learn to listen for information, rather than try to guess and match how many times the teacher's mouth opens and closes.) As students progress, teachers may add their own twists to the marking/scoring procedure. For example, rather than drawing a line on a sheet of paper, students might be instructed to raise and lower their hands, stand when they hear the first pause, sit when they hear the second pause, etc., or count on their fingers. Concentration Plus™ trains students to: tune out distractions, focus on what is being said, follow directions, and practice patience and control. Like any learning technique, it follows a specific progression. Teachers have asked why I tell students to listen for silence first, then for a single word, but not for content. My answer is simple: How can you listen for information and focus on content [a question, instructions, anything], until you first learn to listen—period?

3. As they become adept at listening for pauses, the teacher may add intentional distractions so students must concentrate more on hearing when the pause occurs. Students continue to make a mark when they hear a pause in the reading—but now amid classroom distractions and noise. (Each day a different student is selected to provide the distractions such as whispering, coughing, opening and closing a door, tapping a pencil, scooting a chair, moving around the room, or speaking out—nothing really obnoxious, just natural and annoying.) With distractions, the exercise becomes more challenging and difficult. The students are now having to ignore the distractions while listening for the pauses. We continually tell kids to "just ignore that." Now we're giving them practice while extending their attention span.

4. After students have demonstrated that they can listen for pauses despite distractions, the next step is listening for a particular word. As the teacher continues to read from the lesson content, students now listen for words such as *a, and, to, or, for, from, in, on, of,* or *the.* These are words children tend to unconsciously add or omit when they read, and thus, change the meaning of what they are reading. In this phase of the activity, teachers need to make sure students understand that they are not listening for any pauses; they are only listening for the specific word. (If the specified word is *for,* then students make marks on their papers only when they hear the teacher say the word *for.*) Again, when the teacher senses that most students are fairly accurate at hearing the specified word and marking accordingly, he/she selects a student to provide distractions. The other class members continue listening for the word.

5. Upon mastering instructions 1 through 4, students are ready to extend their listening skills to content information. They now listen for a key word, a main idea, a precise instruction or direction, or a lesson objective. Students listen to what the teacher is reading and mark their papers when they hear the requested information. (Up to this point, students had their eyes closed while they listened for the pause in the reading or the specified word. The teacher may want the eyes to remain closed while the key word is repeated in the reading; otherwise, students should look at the content to see and hear it simultaneously.) They have progressed so that now they are doing three things at once: *listening* for specific information, *looking* at the information, and *making marks* on paper to verify that they heard and saw whatever they were told to listen for. (In addition to listening and concentration, this step helps with word recognition, coordination, processing, reasoning, and analysis. It also reinforces the habit of bringing supplies and materials to class, gets kids to open their books when told, and teaches them to follow directions.)

For instance, the teacher might say, "Class, turn to Chapter 3, section 2, page 45. We're still learning about the Earth. We've listened for the key word, *planet.* The Earth is a planet. It's known as the 'Blue Planet.' On page 45, the main idea will help us understand why the Earth is known as the 'Blue Planet.' Mark your paper when you know why the earth is known as the 'Blue Planet.'"

The teacher reads section 2 aloud. The

students follow the reading silently. When the students think they have heard (and read) the portion of reading that explains why the Earth is called the 'Blue Planet,' they mark their papers just as they have done when they listened for pauses or particular words in the reading. When they mark, they are accountable for knowing the main idea. The reading might go as follows, "Most of Earth looks blue from outer space. The blue color is from Earth's oceans and atmosphere. Oceans cover 70 percent of Earth's surface. Land covers the other 30 percent of Earth. The Earth is different from the other planets because no other planet has such large amounts of water." Students could mark after the first, second, or third sentence— as soon as they understand that oceans are water that look blue and oceans cover most of the Earth; therefore, the Earth looks blue from outer space. If students are listening and looking for main ideas, each main idea should be discussed. Key words, instructions, or specific objectives should be restated after being identified.

6. When students are able to recognize key words and ideas as specified in number 5, they are ready to verbalize information themselves. The teacher tells the students what to listen for, then begins reading. Students mark their papers at the appropriate time. (For example, the teacher may say, "Class, mark your paper when you hear why the Earth is different from other planets." Then he/she reads, "Water makes Earth different from other planets. No other planet has large amounts of water.") The students would draw a line on their papers when they hear, "No other planet has large amounts of water." After students have marked accordingly, the teacher states, "Earth is different from other planets because none of the other planets has large amounts of water." The teacher then signals for the students to repeat the main idea. They do so. The

teacher states the main idea again for emphasis. Step 6 is repeated for as many times as there are main ideas or details to be stressed. (Distractions are no longer necessary since the students are paying attention well enough to respond to a signal from the teacher. The purpose of the distractions in the first place was to get the students to literally try to listen— and, at this point, that goal has been accomplished.)

7. After students are competent with the Concentration Plus™ format, the teacher may wish to use the strategy as a study guide or test review. **As a study guide,** the teacher presents a statement/fact in different questioning formats: a true/false question, a fill-in-the-blank question; *then again* as a matching question. This forces students to think about *what* is being asked as much as *how* it is asked. The teacher asks the question, waits 15 seconds, then says the answer to the question. Next, the teacher asks the same question, waits, signals for the class to respond, then repeats the answer. In order to keep students on their toes and add variety to the game, the teacher can vary the response givers—boys or girls; boys versus girls; those wearing jeans; blue-eyed people; those with short hair, etc. **As a test review,** the teacher should ask the question, wait 15 seconds, then signal the students to answer the question in unison. The teacher repeats the answer. As with the review, students answering the question may vary. Next, the teacher asks the question, but students *write* the answer (younger children or non-writers may circle, underline, or otherwise identify the answer). As usual, the teacher repeats the answer to reinforce the information. If explanations are needed for clarity, the teacher and students discuss the information.

Concentration Plus™ may be extended for longer

than 3 minutes a day. Teachers may continue with the same lesson for several days or use different content. It is a strategy meant to be personalized and adapted to the students' needs. Not all steps must be used on a given day or even used at all. Steps 1 through 4 can be easily used for very young children. Steps 5 through 7 should only be integrated into the routine after students are thoroughly comfortable with Steps 1 through 4. Following are simplified instructions for Concentration Plus™ and examples of possible ways to mark content for repeated use:

Concentration Plus™—Simplified Instructions

Steps 1 through 4 are strictly to help students with listening skills. Steps 5 through 8 teach students to listen for and concentrate on information.

1. Students lower their heads, close their eyes. The teacher reads a selected passage from that day's lesson material. Students make marks on their papers when they hear a pause or hesitation in the reading.

2. Once students become reasonably proficient at listening for pauses, the teacher or an assigned student creates distractions as the teacher reads a selected passage from the daily lesson. The students again listen for and mark their papers each time they hear a pause in the reading.

3. After students learn to listen for pauses, the teacher asks them to listen for a single word such as *a, an, and, of, the, to, or,* or *for* and to make marks on their papers, or signal recognition each time they hear the designated word. When students satisfactorily recognize one word, try another word. The two most difficult words are *a* and *the*. Therefore, begin with another word, such as *for*. (Instead of making marks on paper, teachers may opt to have students count on their fingers, raise or lower their arms, or stand or sit each time they hear the designated word. Students may stand or raise their arms on hearing the first instance of the word and then sit or lower their arms on hearing the subsequent instance, then stand or raise their arms again on the next instance, etc.)

4. Again, when the class proves ready, the teacher or a designated student(s) creates mild distractions. All students aren't going to be 100 percent accurate. Remember, up to and including Step 4, this is only a listening exercise, content is not important. Students must learn first to simply listen and tune out distractions before they are equipped to hear specific information.

5. Next, the teacher has students listen and mark when they hear information such as key words, main ideas, lesson objectives, or instructions, etc. The teacher reads a passage from the day's lesson, waits, then states what the students should hear. If they were to hear a key word, the teacher rereads the content, then states the key word and points out where it appeared in the passage.

6. As the next step in listening mastery, students are ready to learn about verbalizing information themselves. The teacher has the students listen to a passage from the lesson to answer a question,

state the main idea of the passage, pick out details, or provide an explanation, etc. The teacher reads the passage and then states the main idea. He/she then signals for the students to repeat the main idea. After the response, the teacher restates the main idea to avoid misunderstanding.

7. The teacher may use Concentration Plus™ to review or prepare students for testing. A review question is asked. The teacher waits about fifteen seconds, then states the answer. He/she then signals for the class or group to repeat and/or write the answer. The teacher then restates the answer.

8. The teacher should at all times check for understanding and clear up any misunderstanding.

Note: Older students may listen for a variety of content information such as parts of speech—nouns, verbs, pronouns, etc.; context clues, information that is sequentially ordered, information to be summarized, generalities, cause-effect, or for details, etc. Students might count the number of times they hear a word, practice antonyms and synonyms, compare and contrast, draw conclusions, predict outcomes from information heard, and recognize feelings and emotions of characters.

Younger students may listen for letters of the alphabet, phonetically pronounced sounds, colors, names, directions, dates and numbers, etc. Use regular content to cover objectives.

Several examples are given with this and other S.M.A.R.T.S.™ strategies presented in this book. This allows teachers at different grade levels to scan all the examples, or only the most appropriate one for his/her students. Also included are questions and academic objectives with most of the content examples so teachers can see that when a strategy is used, learning occurs and students can be assessed for what they learned by practicing the strategy. The objectives are included because teachers need to use academic objectives when a lesson is being taught, reviewed, and tested. Many schools use work sheets to offer students academic objective practice. If objectives are discussed and practiced with the lesson on a daily basis, students are not shocked to see wording of state-mandated testing. I wrote the poem, "My Clock," for some Kindergarten and first-grade teachers who wanted to use Concentration Plus™ to help their students improve listening skills and attention span, but also to learn about the importance of clocks. In the poem, I provide details describing the minute-hand and the hour-hand, reasons why and how clocks are used, the importance of being able to tell time, the number of minutes in an hour, and the number of hours in the day. These teachers used Concentration Plus™ to work on listening, comprehension, and social skills at the same time.

Elementary and Secondary Examples

Markings in the poem below show the exact way you would mark your own content material in your classroom. The degree of difficulty depends on the grade and ability level of your students. Slash marks denote pauses—in this case twenty-four total. The specified word is underlined. In this case the specified word *to* appears twelve times. The key word, *clock,* is italicized. It appears in the poem four times.

Even though the poem won't win any prizes for writing, I included it because I wanted teachers to know that kids aren't as critical of us as we are of ourselves. Use whatever is needed to help kids learn and improve their skills. Even if poems and stories aren't award-winning, children won't know or care. They'll be learning and having too much fun to notice. Another thing to note is that older students may want to write their own poems, raps, or essays. They can write about anything being studied, mark it the way this poem is marked, and practice it with their parents and friends. We learn best when we teach. Teach students Concentration Plus™ and then let them pass their new knowledge on.

My Clock
by Lauretta Buchanan

(1) I have a *clock.* /
It tells me when /
<u>To</u> go <u>to</u> school
And home again. /

(2) I have a *clock* /
<u>To</u> help make plans. /
<u>To</u> know the time /
I watch the hands. /

(3) Around my *clock* /
The short hand creeps, /
Telling the hours
<u>To</u> wake and sleep. /

(4) The long hand shows the minute. /
It seems almost <u>to</u> fly. /
In only sixty minutes
An hour passes by. /

(5) Sixty minutes make one hour. /
Twenty-four hours make a day. /
It's off <u>to</u> school / and home again, /
Time <u>to</u> work and play. /

6) I use my *clock* <u>to</u> help me /
<u>To</u> go <u>to</u> bed on time, /
So I'll get all the sleep I need, /
<u>To</u> get up / feeling fine! /

How Rocks are Formed—Concentration Plus™ Science

Melted *rock* called magma is found deep within <u>the</u> earth./ When magma comes up through openings in <u>the</u> earth's crust,/ it is called lava./ Lava cools to form hard igneous (IG nee us) *rocks*./ Wind and water break *rocks* into small pieces./ <u>The</u> small pieces settle at <u>the</u> bottom of rivers and oceans./ These layers of sediment harden to form sedimentary (sed uh MEN tuh ree) *rocks*./

Heat and pressure deep inside <u>the</u> earth can cause igneous and sedimentary *rocks* to change./ *Rocks* that are changed are called metamorphic (met uh MOR fik) *rocks*./

There are nine pauses (marked with slashes) in the passage above. The key word rock *appears seven times. The specified word* the *appears five times.*

Questions: How Rocks Are Formed

1. **Magma is _____________ _____________ deep within the earth.**
   Answer: *melted rock*
   Objectives/Expectations: *details; vocabulary; use evidence from simple scientific investigations; distinguish between natural objects and objects made by man.*

2. **When does the magma become lava?**
   Answer: *Magma becomes lava when it comes up through openings in the earth's crust.*
   Objectives/Expectations: *cause/effect; examine how science fosters understanding of issues related to natural resources*

3. **Igneous rocks are nothing but ___________ lava .**
   Answer: *cooled*
   Objectives/Expectations: *logical conclusion; outcome; understand earth's materials*

4. **What two things break rocks into smaller pieces?**
   Answer: *Wind and water break rocks into smaller pieces.*
   Objectives/Expectations: *predict outcome; conclusion; cause/effect; examine the evidence of fossils and organisms that lived long ago*

5. **How are metamorphic rocks formed from igneous and sedimentary rocks?**
   Answer: *Heat and pressure deep inside the earth cause them to change.*
   Objectives/Expectations: *summarization; sequential order; demonstrate how the study of science helps explain changes in environments*

6. **How are sedimentary rocks formed?**
   Answer: *Small pieces of igneous rocks are broken down into little pieces by wind and water and settle at the bottom of rivers and oceans. The layers of sediment harden to form sedimentary rocks.*

Chief Joseph—Concentration Plus™ Social Studies

The story of Chief Joseph and the Nez Perce
Taken from *The Biography of a Great Indian,* Wilson-Erickson, 1936

The Nez Perce Indians originally lived <u>in</u> the region where Idaho, Oregon, and Washington State meet/ —<u>in</u> the Wallowa Valley area./ Nez Perce means pierced nose./ The most widely known Nez Perce Indian was Chief *Joseph,*/ whose Indian name was Hin-mah-too-yah-lat-kekt./ Translated, this means Thunder Rolling Down the Mountains./ Chief *Joseph's* father,/ referred to by his Christian name as *Joseph* the Elder,/ was one of the first Nez Perce converts to Christianity./ *Joseph* the Elder was an active supporter of the tribe's long-standing peace with the white man./ In 1855, he helped Washington's territorial governor set up a Nez Perce reservation that stretched from Oregon into Idaho./ However, <u>in</u> 1863,/ prospectors overran the Nez Perce reservation after discovering gold there,/ and the federal government took back almost six million acres of this land./ The government restricted the tribe to a reservation <u>in</u> Idaho that was one-tenth the size of their prior reservation./ *Joseph* the Elder,/ feeling betrayed,/ destroyed his Bible and American flag, and refused to move from the Nez Perce homeland or to sign the treaty that would have made the new boundaries official./

Chief *Joseph,*/ who was designated Chief upon *Joseph* the Elder's death <u>in</u> 1871,/ inherited this volatile situation./ <u>In</u> 1873, a federal order had seemed likely to remove white settlers and to let the Nez Perce remain, which would have calmed the situation./ But/ the federal government reversed itself and fighting broke out between the Nez Perce and U.S. troops;/the year was 1877./ *Joseph's* warriors won several battles,/ but he realized they could not defeat the Army,/ led by General Howard./ Chief *Joseph* ordered a retreat of the Nez Perce to Canada./ He conducted the retreat so skillfully that he has been called the "Indian Napoleon."/ Even the U.S. Army was impressed with the 1,400-mile march./ The retreat ended with Chief *Joseph* surrendering just miles from the Canadian border./ Following is Chief *Joseph's* well-known 1877 speech when he surrendered in the Bear Paw Mountains./

" I am tired of fighting./ Our chiefs are killed./ Looking Glass is dead./ Toohoolhoolzote is dead./ The old men are all dead./ It is the young men who say,/ 'Yes' or 'No.'/ He who led the young men (Olikut) is dead./ It is cold,/ and we have no blankets./ The little children are freezing to death./ My people,/ some of them,/ have run away to the hills,/ and have no blankets,/ no food./ No one knows where they are –/ perhaps freezing to death./ I want to have time to look for my children,/ and see how many of them I can find./ Maybe I shall find them among the dead./ Hear me,/ my chiefs!/ I am tired./ My heart is sick and sad./ From where the sun now stands I will fight no more forever."/

In the passage above there are fifty-nine pauses. The word <u>in</u> *appears eight times. The key word* <u>Joseph</u> *appears eleven times.*

School Bus Safety—Concentration Plus™ Language Arts

Riding <u>the</u> school *bus* is a safe way to get to school and home again if you follow some simple safety rules./

Get to <u>the</u> *bus* stop early,/ and wait with other children if you can./

Remember that <u>the</u> *bus* is surrounded by a danger zone./ This is an area all around <u>the</u> *bus* where <u>the</u> driver can't see you./ <u>The</u> driver can't see children who are too close to <u>the</u> *bus*./ You can escape from <u>the</u> danger zone by taking 5 giant steps away from <u>the</u> *bus*./

When you get on <u>the</u> *bus* always use <u>the</u> handrail./ Take your seat quickly./ Pay attention to what <u>the</u> *bus* driver says./ Keep your arms and hands inside <u>the</u> *bus*, /and don't stand up until <u>the</u> *bus* stops./

When you are getting off <u>the</u> *bus* wait your turn,/ and use <u>the</u> handrail./ Then take 5 giant steps away from <u>the</u> *bus*./ Never bend down near or under <u>the</u> *bus*./ Don't go back to pick up anything you dropped near <u>the</u> *bus*,/ or left on <u>the</u> *bus*./

When you cross <u>the</u> street, always cross in front of <u>the</u> *bus* so <u>the</u> driver can see you./

In the passage above are nineteen pauses. The word <u>the</u> *appears twenty-three times. The key word* <u>bus</u> *appears sixteen times.*

Proteins—Concentration Plus™ Health

Proteins are chemical compounds that are an essential part of every cell./ Living things require *proteins* to stay alive because these compounds repair cells and build new tissue./ *Proteins* are large molecules that consist of chains of <u>amino acids</u>,/ which are also chemical compounds./ There are about 20 kinds of <u>amino acids</u>./ Our bodies use these relatively few <u>amino acids</u> to make thousands of different *proteins*./ <u>Amino acids</u> are the building blocks of *proteins*./ Our bodies can make 12 of the <u>amino acids</u>,/ but the other 8 are obtained from what we eat./

Most of the flesh of animals and most of the living matter in plants are *proteins*./ Foods of high *protein* value include red meat,/ fish,/ poultry,/ dairy products and eggs./ These foods also contain all the <u>amino acids</u> needed by the body./ Many of the plant *proteins* are missing one or more essential <u>amino acids</u>./ People who are vegetarians must be careful to include a variety of plant foods so they receive all the essential <u>amino acids</u>./

Ingested *proteins* are broken down in the digestive system into <u>amino acids</u>./ The <u>amino acids</u> are then absorbed into the blood,/ and carried to all organs and tissues where they are rebuilt into new body *proteins* by the cells./ Different cells make a different range of *proteins*. /The genes within each cell instruct the cells which *proteins* to manufacture./

In the passage above there are twenty-two pauses. The word <u>protein</u> *appears twelve times. The key words* <u>amino acid</u> *appear ten times.*

Decimal Basics – Concentration Plus™ Math

1. First,/ it's important to understand *decimal* place-value./ Look at the <u>numbers</u> below./

0./	4 /	5 /	8 /	9 /
ones/	tenths/	hundredths/	thousandths /	ten-thousandths/

This <u>number</u> is read four thousand,/ five hundred eighty-nine ten-thousandths/

2. The places to the right of the *decimal* point are *decimal* places./
Practice listening to and reading other <u>numbers</u>:/

0.9	=	nine tenths/
0.23	=	twenty-three one hundredths/
0.752	=	seven hundred fifty-two thousandths /

3. Often *decimals* are read and said another way./ You can read 0.4589 as "point four five eight nine"./ The <u>number</u> 10.236 can be read as "ten and two hundred thirty-six thousandths,"/ or as "ten point two three six."/

4. It is important to know how to multiply *decimals*./ First is an example of multiplying a whole <u>number</u> by a *decimal*./

```
   $1.45     Notice that there are the same number of decimal places in the product as
  x  23      in the decimal factor ($1.45)./ Whenever a decimal is multiplied by a whole
 ------      number,/ the product will have the same number of decimal places as the
   4 35      decimal factor./
  29 0
 ------
  $33.35
```

5. When a *decimal* is multiplied by a *decimal*,/ the product has the same <u>number</u> of *decimal* places as the total <u>number</u> of *decimal* places in both factors./

```
   5.697     Notice that the numbers 5.697 and 4.11 have a total of 5 decimal places. /
 x  4.11     Notice also that the product of the two numbers also has five decimal places./
   5697      You multiply without worrying about the decimals;/ then, /after you have
   5697      calculated the product—/ count five places from the right and place the
  22788      decimal point./
 --------
 23.41467
```

6. It is easy to multiply *decimals* by 10,/ 100 or 1000./ All you have to do is move the *decimal* point./ Look at these examples./

10 x 9.651 = 96.51
When multiplying a *decimal* by 10,/ move the *decimal* point one place to the right./

100 x 9.651 = 965.1
When multiplying a *decimal* by 100,/ move the *decimal* point two places to the right./

1000 x 9.651 = 9651
When multiplying a *decimal* by 1000,/ move the *decimal* point three places to the right./

7. Dividing *decimals* by whole <u>numbers</u> is simple./ The *decimal* point in the quotient is placed above the *decimal* point in the dividend./ Look at the example below./

$$12 \overline{) 48.000} = 4.000$$

Notice how the *decimal* is lined up./

8. Dividing *decimals* by 10,/100 or 1000 is not hard./ Simply move the *decimal* point./ Look at these examples./

673.4 ÷ 10 = 67.34
When dividing a *decimal* by 10, /just move its *decimal* point one place to the left./

673.4 ÷ 100 = 6.734
When dividing a *decimal* by 100,/ move its *decimal* point two places to the left./

673.4 ÷ 1000 = 0.6734
When dividing a *decimal* by 1000,/ just move its *decimal* point three places to the left./

9. Often you will be asked to round a *decimal*./ You will be asked to round to the nearest tenth,/ one hundredth or one thousandth./ Below are examples of rounding./

To the nearest tenth – / 25.6915 would round to 25.7/

To the nearest one hundredth - / 25.6915 would round to 25.69/

To the nearest one thousandth - / 25.6915 would round to 25.692/

In the passage above there are seventy-one pauses. The word <u>number</u> appears thirteen times. The key word <u>decimal</u> appears forty times.

Concentration Plus™

What Is a Friend?—Concentration Plus™ Language Arts

What is a *friend?*/ A *friend* helps you get up when you fall down./ A *friend* helps you pick up your toys./ A *friend* shares cookies,/ toys,/ <u>and</u> chocolate milk./ A *friend* doesn't mean to make you cry,/ <u>and</u> says he's sorry if he does./ A *friend* will never lie/ <u>and</u> will always tell you the truth./ A *friend* plays fairly/ <u>and</u> takes turns./ A *friend* likes you,/ <u>and</u> is even nicer to you when you're sad./

In the passage above there are fourteen pauses. The word <u>and</u> appears five times. The key word <u>friend</u> appears eight times.

Questions: What is a Friend?

1. **What does a friend do when you fall down?**
    Answer: *helps you get up*
    Objectives/Expectations: *feelings and relationships; cause/effect; logical conclusion*

2. **List three things a friend might share with you.**
    Answer: *cookies, toys, chocolate milk*
    Objectives/Expectations: *actions and outcomes; details; fact/opinion*

3. **Yes or No? A friend plays fairly and takes turns.**
    Answer: *Yes*
    Objectives/Expectations: *relationships and feelings of characters; outcome*

4. **What might a friend help you pick up after you've been playing?**
    Answer: *toys*
    Objectives/Expectations: *predict outcome; logical conclusion; inference*

5. **What does a friend do if he makes you cry?**
    Answer: *Says I'm sorry.*
    Objectives/Expectations: *predict outcome; logical outcome*

CHAPTER 2

LOOK IT UP!™

OR

"This Is the Last Time I'm Telling You to Open That Book!"

How many times have you asked your students to open their books to a certain page and at least two or three make no attempt whatsoever? The faces and names of those students come to mind almost instantly. Those are the kids who are physically present in your classroom, but mentally somewhere else. Those are the ones who, no matter how young or how old they are, either aren't listening, don't care, are completely lost, or have already given up on you, themselves, and school. You've asked the class to turn to page 63. It's a pretty safe bet some of your little darlings aren't going to get whiplash reaching for their books.

Some may not even know where their books are. If they do, turning to page 63 is way down on their "to do" list. If this notion conjures up images in your mind, it's probably because predicaments like this are a daily occurrence in most classrooms. It gets under our skin when we're ignored. We're not prepared for this feeling of losing control, of being challenged. It's humiliating. We don't picture other teachers being treated this way. We take it personally. Especially when we think back to what it was like when we were in school. We wouldn't have dared to treat a teacher like this. Teachers were revered. They were admired. Back in my day, the boys wanted to be doctors and firemen. The girls wanted to be nurses and teachers. When I was in school, we looked up to our teachers—not away from them. I would like to have been a teacher *back in my day.*

Back in my day, we did what the teacher said because getting into trouble in school meant double trouble at home. In my children's day, the teachers' authority seemed to be dwindling, boundaries were tested, and the word *respect* didn't mean as much as it had *back in my day.* Today, it's even tougher to be a teacher. The attitude is "Make me," instead of "Help me," "Let me," or "Show me." The joy of teaching has to be intrinsic instead of extrinsic. Often the thrill has to come from our inner voice saying "Good job," instead of somebody else saying "Thank you." Satisfaction has to come from knowing who we help rather than from the gratitude of those we help.

As head teacher in a psychiatric hospital, I've been there. I've stayed up until 3 a.m. making out final exams only to find the kids checked out ADA (against doctor's approval) the next morning. In other schools, I've stayed to tutor kids who have never shown up. I've wondered why on earth I'm grading papers after midnight or spending three hours writing a test my students will finish in thirty minutes. But, truth be known, I'm doing it because it's my life's work. It's what I was born to do and what I choose to do—and I sincerely believe that if we're teaching for any other reason than that we were born to do it, then we really should think about another profession. I probably need to apologize here for getting preachy and philosophical on this subject, but it is serious stuff. My feelings are especially strong about this.

Although I don't pretend to have seen or done it all, I've had my good days and my bad, and when I ask students to do something, I really, really, really want them to do it. I doubt I'm the only teacher who feels this way. Giving instruc-tions and being ignored must be one of the problems that has jaws tightening around the globe. In response to this dilemma, the Look It Up!™ strategy emerged victorious, and attacked lack of motivation, too! It's one of the best techniques I've ever seen for getting kids actively involved in a lesson. I can say this because it evolved. I didn't just think, "Well, I believe the world needs for me to create something wonderful. Let's see. Ah, yes. I'll write a teaching strategy, pick up the cleaning, and go to the grocery store when I get off work. I do have, after all, twelve undesignated minutes." No, the strategy came together out of a need, improved bit by bit, and has grown through trial and lots of error.

The Look It Up!™ title isn't especially profound. We've all said, "Look it up," scads of times when kids wanted us to give them the answer. They don't really care what the answer is as long as it's given to them. Being determined they're going to learn by doing, we're not about to give an answer when it's right there in the book and they can look it up. At any rate, that was my attitude.

As I've gotten older, I've actually realized that sometimes it's really okay to give kids an answer. Maybe it's because I'm mellowing. Maybe I'm maturing. Maybe it's because I've needed information and didn't have a clue where to find it, like when you do spell check on the computer and you misspell the word so badly the computer tells you "no suggestion." It is times like that when it would be nice for someone to simply tell me the answer. But I still think we—kids, whoever—should look stuff up. I've just realized during my "wizening" period that "gray" happens as often as "black and white."

Back to the birth and development of Look It Up:™ I'd tell my kids to open their books to a particular page. Twenty-nine would. Three wouldn't. They weren't mean or bad . . . they just didn't want to open their books. I'd wait a couple of minutes (just in case they needed time to process what I'd said), then I would repeat it again. By now, this little tinge of frustration and tension would begin to move up to my neck, so I'd say, "I said, 'Open your books to page 63.' Do it now please." Then, I'd back off and wait. I probably could have waited until the next millennium and nothing would have happened. After a while, I always became sufficiently ticked off and hurt. The students who weren't minding probably didn't notice my agitation, and if they did, they didn't care. Ultimately, my facial expression turned into a scowl, my voice volume escalated and took on a tremor, and my body began to resemble a German commando. The unopened books remained unopened. With patience wearing thin, I'd direct them to immediately turn to page 63, exclaiming this was the last time I was going to tell them to do it. In the end, even as I went from desk to desk opening books to page 63, I'd comment, "Don't expect me to do that for you again." They knew I would. I knew I would. There would be a next time and a next and a next . . . and there were. . . until I'd had enough. I decided I didn't have the time or the patience to open students' books all day long. It's exhausting to partake in a battle of wills all day, every day. It's not worth it. I eventually gave up and wised up. I invented a reading game where kids have a blast opening their books, reading passages from them, and even analyzing what they read. It was refreshingly wonderful.

When books are distributed at the beginning of school, I'm fairly sure the intent is for them to be opened and used. They don't have to be studied cover to cover—in fact most shouldn't be. Telling kids to read a chapter and answer the questions time after time is one of the things that turns kids off of school. When kids sometimes hear the words "section review" or "problem set," their motivation switches off and they either head for automatic pilot or to somewhere else in the brain that is far, far away from the topic at hand.

The saving grace for kids is they are basically curious creatures. Good teaching and books with pictures (seriously) hook into that curiosity and with luck keep them inquisitive. The good teaching part helps kids know where and how to look for information. Good teaching enables them to continually want to know more and learn more, with one thing leading to another in the quest for more.

Books offer the "more" part. When we encourage reading and help students develop the ability to take words from the printed page and turn them into visual

images in their mind's eye, we move them further and further away from helplessness and closer and closer to independence. Since being self-reliant is a primary goal of education and since learning is a natural, integral part of a child's life, opening a book is certainly an important step.

In Look It Up!™ opening the book is one of the strategy's elements the students like best. I don't know why. I don't know if it's the idea that it's a game, or it's the competition, or what. I just know they open their books willingly and eagerly. I know they laugh—and learn—and are actively involved in the lesson when they're playing it. As a parent and teacher, that's good enough for me. To see kids get caught up in procedures that are teaching them to listen, follow directions, locate information, reason, and actually proof their work is a vision to my eyes and brings a tightening in my heart. Even kids who are hesitant or shy jump into the action. It's an opportunity for painless instruction and fast paced fun. When my students ask to play Look It Up!,™ a game that teaches both academic and behavioral skills, my tension takes a hike and you can color me happy.

It's amazing what the feeling of success can do. It's sort of like labor pains and birth—you know there were some tough times, but things are so good right now you can't quite remember the hurt. I think that's what keeps us coming back to teaching. Knowing that on that good day, when everything is clicking, when there is real learning going on—in the end, we really do make a difference. Look It Up!™ helps my kids—and me—have a good day. When we play it, there's learning going on.

S.M.A.R.T.S.™ Look It Up!™

S.M.A.R.T.S.™ Look It Up!™ is a teaching strategy specifically designed to improve behavior as well as the ability to locate, process, and comprehend written information. Students practice research skills, learn to formulate ideas, and explain information in their own words to ensure complete understanding. Look It Up!™ is an excellent tool for introducing new material, review, or for test preparation. It incorporates academic and behavioral skills, and lets students practice both as the game is being played. I use either Concentration Plus™ or Look It Up!™ to begin each class using daily objectives, specific content, or content information in need of further discussion or remediation S.M.A.R.T.S.™ strategies may be used with any content, so use it with whatever you teach. Remember, I'm giving you examples. I know the S.M.A.R.T.S.™ games. You know your content. You're the expert in your subject, not I. So tailor this game to your content and needs.

Look It Up!™ is an activity specifically intended to help students enhance the use of written materials; expand thinking, generalization, and summarization skills; bolster the ability to compare and contrast and validate reasoning; improve the use of math operations and procedures; make following directions habitual; and practice appropriate social interaction.

1. Each student is responsible for having a copy of the book or other printed material being used.

2. Students may look on with other team members, but may not go to get any forgotten books. Having the book is a critical component of Look It Up!™ Opening it when the teacher says "Go," is one of the things kids like best about the game. It also teaches students to be responsible and to come to class prepared. Consequently, having a book is important to the student who has his/her book as well as to the student who does not. The student with the book is relieved and eager to play. The student without a book wishes he/she had his/hers. I've found that going without a book for several days prods the student's memory, successfully encourages responsibility, and lets everyone enjoy the game 100%. Most of what we do in life is habitual. Shouldn't our jobs as parents and teachers be helping kids develop good habits that will let them move successfully through life? I think so.

3. Students are divided into groups of four to six. The teacher always assigns the members of each group and determines the role or job of each student within the group. The groups' makeup should be as evenly distributed as possible. Groups should remain the same for the duration of play. If the activity lasts for two class periods, the groups should stay the same for the two class periods. Teachers may assign groups by the activity or for a specified length of time. When keeping the same groups for a particular amount of time, I have found one week is best. My reasoning is thus: If you change group membership every day or even every few days, you're wasting valuable teaching time while kids are getting organized into their groups. If groups consist of the same people for more than a week, they tend to get tired of each other and sometimes feel saddled with other students. You don't want to push kids to the point they complain about being with each other. They can and should get used to being with whomever is assigned to their group, but remember — patience is learned. Don't test it too often. Most people can tolerate and adapt to anyone or anything for a little while but shouldn't be pushed to their limits unnecessarily.

4. The teacher appoints a different student as group teacher each class period or day. This student will signal the readiness of the team and may be called on to be the spokesperson for the team. I should point out here that two things in my classroom never change: The first is that team leaders are called "group teacher" because the initials of "group teacher" are "GT" (gifted and talented). All children deserve to be "GT" at some point in their lives. The other is that no students argue with me about their team or job assignment, complain, or ask to change. Even though groups change weekly, as a rule, jobs within the group change every day. Every student in the class will get to be group teacher. Every student will probably be with someone he or she doesn't like. Every student knows his or her circumstances won't be forever. Kids have to learn to work with whomever they're with and make the best of every situation. It's called "life." If we're going to expect something from students, we have to first teach it. Next, we help them practice it. And finally, when they've learned it, *then* we can expect it.

5. After assigning the groups, the teacher instructs students to open their books to a particular page (to what is being studied), and turn the books over, placing them face down on their desks, or by placing bookmarks (or

strips of paper) at the beginning and at the end of the pages to be looked in and studied.

6. Once the books are face down on the top of the desks, students must place their open hands palms down on top of the books in front of them. They remain this way until the teacher asks a question or gives an instruction and says "Go!"

7. When the teacher says, "Go!" the books are turned over and the students look for the answer to the question. (If books are turned face down, students listen to the questions more readily and aren't as tempted to cheat by getting a head start. If they are holding their books or have the content facing upward, they want to beat everyone else, and tend to open the books before the teacher says "Go." When they do this, they're not listening to the question or for directions—two of the reasons kids fail tests. If students turn all their attention toward the question and refrain from opening their books ahead of time, they give themselves a much better chance of understanding exactly what is being asked so they'll know exactly what it is they're looking for.)

8. In order for a team to be called on to answer a question, it must follow explicit rules. If anyone on a team does not comply with all of the rules, that team will not be called on for that particular question.

Use the above-mentioned instructions to ready students for play and note that the simplified instructions 9 through 17 deal specifically with behavior. Numbers 18 through 22 deal with other instructions and aspects of the strategy.

9. All team members must participate in locating the answer. Peer pressure from team members when a team is not called on for lack of participation usually gives noncompliant students the "encouragement" to get involved.

10. Hands stay in place until the teacher says "Go." Then everyone looks for the answer.

11. Team members show the answer and location of the answer to the group teacher and to each other until everyone in the group knows both the answer location and the correct response well enough to explain if called upon.

12. The group teacher raises his/her hand without making a sound or leaving his/her seat, only when everyone on the team knows the answer and where the answer is located. Only then is the team completely ready to answer the question.

13. The teacher calls on the first group teacher who raises his/her hand, assuming that team has followed all of the rules.

14. The teacher asks the location of the answer.

15. If the location is incorrect, the teacher says, "Thank you very much," and moves to another group for the answer.

16. If the location is correct, the group teacher, or whomever the teacher selects from the team may begin to answer.

17. If the teacher can tell the answer is going to be incorrect, the teacher immediately stops the answer by saying, "Thank you very much," and calls on another group teacher to answer. When this happens, students should realize one of three things: (a) the location of the answer is correct;

(b) the answer is incorrect; or (c) the question was not answered the way it was asked, e.g., "Read me the passage that explains . . ." or "Describe how the passage showed . . . ." The teacher initially tells the students not to close their books when someone else is called on. If they do, the natural consequence is that they will rarely, if ever, be the first group to locate the answer.

18. If the group teacher or selected group member states/reads the correct answer, the teacher acknowledges the answer and the team can then say where the hands are to be placed while the next question is being read. The two incentives students find most exciting about Look It Up!™ which keep them actively participating are: getting to open the book when they hear the word "Go!," and getting to say where the hands are to be placed (e.g., on top of the head, sit on them, on their knees, on the floor, etc.) while the next question is being read.

19. If the answer is incorrect, other teams have the opportunity to follow the above instructions and answer the question.

20. If none of the teams finds the answer, the teacher tells the class the location of the answer. Teams must then find the answer per the teacher's instructions. Then the teacher calls on the group teacher to read the answer.

21. If necessary, the teacher and class members discuss the answer prior to the next question.

22. If the teacher chooses to award points, a team may earn 5 points for finding the answer, following directions, and reading the answer. The team must correctly complete all three assignments to receive the points. If no one finds the answer and the teacher reveals the location of the answer, no points are given. During the discussion however, the teacher may award 2 points to each team who appropriately participates in the discussion.

Note: I don't usually award points. Students need to know that they don't always "get" something for everything they do. There are times when they need to do something simply because it's the right thing to do.

I will offer several different types of content for Look It Up!™ examples below. Some will be for elementary students, others for secondary. Most will be actual material I have summarized from various texts.

The following is an essay I wrote for a Behavioral Conference. I'm including it for several reasons: 1) people always ask what to do in certain behavioral situations, 2) teachers often find these suggestions helpful in their classrooms, 3) I want to illustrate that Look It Up!™ works with any content, and 4) the questions at the conclusion of the essay demonstrate that learning objectives may be applied to any content. If objectives are tied to and taught to students on a daily basis through lecture, discussion, or questioning, students will learn more easily, improve comprehension, and improve critical thinking and analytical skills. In other words, by using objective learning to teach students how to learn, information is more thoroughly processed, and recall and understanding are greatly enhanced.

Working on Behavior—Look It Up!™

by Lauretta Buchanan

In nearly every school I visit, teachers tell me that behavior is getting in the way of learning. Whether it's lashing out, acting out, attention getting behavior, power struggles, disruptions, or anger, misbehavior is a common problem in most classrooms. Too many teachers are dog tired and disenchanted with teaching. Too many students are unmotivated, frustrated, and failing. Some of them are just waiting until they're old enough to drop out. I can probably describe almost any misbehavior, with certain kids I have known coming to mind. Our kids, teachers, and schools need "fixin'." We have a lot of work to do and we need to do it together. Let's start now.

When kids are angry or hurt, they tend to lash out at other students, at anyone in authority and even at people who have done nothing to them at all. Whether the hurt is real or imagined—and most of it is all too real—anger from that hurt manifests itself in power struggles, frustration, and behavior that is meant to get a reaction. Angry kids pick fights, push, bump, hit, vandalize, cry, curse, yell, criticize, find fault, blame, manipulate, pout, seethe, shut out, turn off, and give up on everybody else, and especially on themselves. They can be exhausting to teach, difficult to like, and troublesome to the point that we wonder why in the world we chose this job in the first place, and why we keep coming back to it day after day. Angry kids bother us. They hurt our feelings. They hurt our hearts. They stretch, shred, and exhaust our patience and emotions. But they need us—*desperately.*

Angry kids must be dealt with unemotionally, in the present. Don't bring up what they did yesterday. Yesterday's gone. Let it go. Don't lecture them. Don't judge them. Just help them save face, settle down, keep from going from bad to worse, and control emotions that could get them kicked out, beaten up, or worse. With these kids, we somehow have to remain friendly while being firm, stay calm while being insistent, and communicate while tempers are cooling and more congenial actions are being considered.

Dealing with kids who are angry and hurt is tiring. It drains us physically, mentally, and emotionally. I watch teachers use every ounce of their strength to quietly extinguish a child's angry flashes and think to myself, "These people really are grossly underpaid." But then, can you actually put a dollar figure on working miracles?

Next, let's tackle attention-getting behavior and wipe it off the face of the earth. On second thought, that's not likely to happen, so I'll just touch on a few things that may help and move on. Everyone I know, including me, needs attention. We just go about getting attention differently from the way kids do. We usually do it the right way. Kids haven't figured that out yet. They think they can do something and voila! They get what they want.

Regardless of whether they're disrupting class, or simply doing (or not doing) something, some kids feel that negative attention—reprimands or call downs—is better than no attention at all. We've got to show them that positive attention—recognition or acknowledgment—is more fruitful. Sometimes when a kid doesn't get what he wants, doesn't get the attention sought, or gets bored because nobody is paying any attention, he or she will give up and stop the behavior. Sometimes when the attention is overtly given to somebody else, the attention getting behavior stops or at least dissipates.

One of the most distressing things about these kids is they're the ones who pull other kids into the commotion and put a real kink in our plans. In trying to deal with the behavior, you can't buy into their acting out. We can freeze them with "The Look," position ourselves in "The Stance," or petrify them with "The Touch." We can do these without missing a beat in the lesson. But move in close to be really effective. Also, try "The Overlook." During "The Overlook," you move right up next to the kid who is acting out, overtly ignore him or her, and blatantly acknowledge another student like he or she is a long-lost, dearly-beloved friend. This is a real "chapper" to the student being ignored.

Do whatever works. Try different things, but don't use a student's name if he or she is misbehaving. Say the name when you're praising or encouraging a child—not during a reprimand. Try giving a signal as a reminder or prompt. Try silence, or a simple "no," or "stop." Ask a specific question to pull the misbehaving student into the lesson. Just don't tell the kid what he or she already knows such as, "Susie, you're talking again." Chances are, smooth-talkin' little Susie hasn't shut her mouth since birth. To begin with, you're telling her what she already knows she's doing, and then you direct everybody's attention to her, which is what Susie Q. wanted all along.

It's tough to know what to do. Whatever you do, don't act rashly and don't let it show if you're ticked. If you do, the kid has the satisfaction of getting your goat, along with the attention of the other kids. Sometimes it's helpful to remember that I'm being paid to be there and the kid isn't. Sometimes it's comforting to know that when all is said and done, my hand holds the all-powerful grade book. And sometimes I remember what I'm doing there to begin with: I'm a teacher. I'm trying to get these kids ready for life after schooling.

As far as power struggles go, I say, "Don't do it. You can't win." Don't buy into this behavior because it'll cost you in the long run. Power **IS** a powerful thing! Everybody wants it. People do ridiculous things to get it and even more ridiculous stuff to show they've gotten it. People argue, become passive-aggressive, puff up, act stubborn, have to be right, turn violent, do any number of unnecessary, egotistical things to get power—just to show you they can. Kids may not work in class, or turn in homework, or follow your directions. They may decide to do nothing but sit and be totally indifferent. Sometimes they give you their "Look." Their "Look" is quite a bit different from our "Look." Theirs isn't like the one Rasheed Wallace kept giving the referee during the Portland–Lakers play off game of '99. That "Look" was an "I'm going to wipe the floor with you (clean version), you little, short zebra; I could buy and sell twenty of you, you twerp (clean version)" look. Rasheed got his second technical foul for his "look" and got kicked out of the game. Nope, the one our kids give us when they're being passive says, "I don't care, you boring dork; I'm not listening to you anyway." One more time: you're the adult. You're bigger (maybe), smarter, older, wiser, dedicated, professional, wonderful, and loving. You're too bright to fall into their traps, so don't do it.

If, however, the passive power struggle becomes explosive, then that's another story. If this is the case, you've got to defuse this tedious, potentially dangerous crap shoot immediately if not sooner. Here, you stay outwardly calm. Be unemotional but caring. Continue to stay focused on the student. Listen intently to what is being said and to what is *not* being said, and resolve to avoid an argument or blow up at all costs. Think about this: If you are "in control" you don't have to be "controlling."

Even though power struggles seem personal, they're usually not and you're not the real target or the real problem. In fact, you're probably just the one who happens to be there—and thank goodness you are. If we weren't "there" for a lot of our kids, some of them would never have anybody there for them at all, and being "there" all by yourself is an awfully lonely place to be.

Finally, I want to acknowledge that every one of us has experienced frustration, anxiety, or the fear of failure. Most of us have probably behaved badly at least once. I've acted out a couple of times myself. I did it in school. I've done it with my kids and I do it with my beloved husband on a semi-regular basis. I did it growing up and I still do it now. In fact, I've written a little ditty about my occasional lack of serenity and tranquility. It's called "Losin' It."

Losin' It
by Lauretta Buchanan

Whether on the road or with my friends,
I do it time and time again.

Both in the car and on a plane,
I do it, then I feel insane.

If in a store, or if in school,
I do it like a first rate fool.

It's with my peers and cleaning house,
Or when I'm sick or just a louse.

I do it way too much it seems…
Sometimes my insides have to scream.

My temper fits, I do not choose…
But the older I get—the shorter my fuse.

Anyway, the deal is this: We lose our cool. Kids lose their cool. The objective is to learn to deal with frustration and anxiety by taking a deep breath, thinking, regaining our composure, and having the courage to start over [and over and over]. Real failure is the failure to try again. Our problem with our kids (at home as well as at school) is that they're too young to know all the stuff we know, to have the wisdom we have, or to have lived through the messes we've worked ourselves into and out of. I believe it's called experience. In certain areas, but not many, age does have its rewards. Little things aren't as "life altering" at fifty-six as they were at sixteen. Yep, we're the adults here. We're the ones who understand that bad things make the good things better. We're blessed to have lived long enough that we can look back to help kids move ahead. Our task is to teach self-talk, reasoning, patience, and control. Our charge is to teach by example, show the grace God gives to us, and demonstrate forgiveness and understanding. Our job is to practice the career we chose, but to be smart enough to leave as much of the job as possible at work. It's silly to think we can help kids or anybody else unless we're okay ourselves. Whether we read, walk, work out, cook, watch TV, take a bubble bath, pull weeds, plant flowers, or watch the grass grow, we have to take care of ourselves before we can take care of them. Laugh, cry, hug, reach out, ask for help. Do whatever it takes to get through the bad days, celebrate the good ones, and appreciate the difference. When I think about it, my life could be a whole lot worse. Couldn't yours?

Questions: Working on Behavior

1. **In most schools, what gets in the way of learning?**
   Answer: *Behavior; p. 28, left column.*

   Objectives/Expectations: *Cause/effect; main idea; predict outcome*

2. **How should we deal with angry students?**
   Answer: *Unemotionally; in the present; firmly, calmly, without lecturing or judging; by helping the student save face, settle down, and get control; p. 28, bottom left, top right column*

   Objectives/Expectations: *Feelings/emotions; supporting details; analysis*

3. **What are four instances that may cause students to stop attention-getting behavior?**
   Answer: *(1) when the child doesn't get what he/she wants (2) when the child doesn't get attention (3) if he/she becomes bored (4) when another child overtly gets the attention in spite of what the misbehaving child is doing; page 28, bottom right column.*

   Objectives/Expectations: *Listing; predicting; outcome; logical conclusion*

4. **A. Name four actions teachers use (other than verbally correcting students) to deal with attention getting behavior.**
   Answer: *(1) "The Look" (2) "The Stance" (3) "The Touch" (4) "The Overlook;" p. 29.*

   B. Which is probably the most commonly used?
   Answer: *"The Look," p. 29, first mentioned, most familiar to educators.*

   Objectives/Expectations: *Compare and contrast; relationships; cause/effect*

5. **Explain why you don't use the student's name during a reprimand.**
   Answer: *You don't use a student's name during a reprimand because the use of the name calls attention to the student. If the student is trying to get attention in the first place, you'd be playing right into the student's hands; p. 29, left column.*

   Objectives/Expectations: *Summarization; critical thinking; cause/effect*

6. **Why is a power struggle a "no-win" situation for the teacher?**
   Answer: *As a rule, the student tries to entice the teacher and pull him/her into the struggle. The power struggle could be an argument, class disruption for attention, passive-aggressive behavior, or not following directions. Whatever the student does, he/she is trying to get a*

reaction from the teacher. If the teacher gets involved and shows irritation, the student has won the struggle because of the reaction. The student then feels in control, because the teacher "bought into" the power struggle. It's a one-upmanship thing; p. 29, right column.

Objectives/Expectations: *Summarization; relationships; cause/effect; inference; vocabulary*

7. **How might a teacher's frustration, anxiety, and/or fear of failure be manifested?**
Answer: *Temper tantrums; "losing your cool;" p. 30, left column.*
Objectives/Expectations: *Cause/effect; outcomes*

8. **What are some tactics we might try if we become frustrated or anxious?**
Answer: *Take a deep breath, think rationally, start over, use self-talk; p. 30, bottom.*
Objectives/Expectations: *Logical reasoning; predict outcomes*

9. **What must we do for ourselves so we can help others?**
Answer: *Take care of ourselves/Do whatever it takes to be okay ourselves; p. 31, top.*
Objectives/Expectations: *Cause/effect; logical reasoning*

10. **If a student is becoming explosive, how might we respond?**
Answer: *Stay calm, show we care but be unemotional, focus on the student, listen; p. 29, right column.*
Objectives/Expectations: *Details; critical thinking; logical reasoning; cause/effect*

Chief Joseph—Look It Up!™ Social Studies

The story of Chief Joseph and the Nez Perce
Taken from *The Biography of a Great Indian*, Wilson-Erickson, 1936

The Nez Perce Indians originally lived in the region where Idaho, Oregon, and Washington State meet – in the Wallowa Valley area. Nez Perce means pierced nose. The most widely-known Nez Perce Indian was Chief Joseph, whose Indian name was Hin-mah-too-yah-lat-kekt. Translated, this means Thunder Rolling Down the Mountains. Chief Joseph's father, referred to by his Christian name as Joseph the Elder, was one of the first Nez Perce converts to Christianity. Joseph the Elder was an active supporter of the tribe's long-standing peace with the white man. In 1855, he helped Washington's territorial governor set up a Nez Perce reservation that stretched from Oregon into Idaho. However, in 1863, prospectors overran the Nez Perce reservation after discovering gold there, and the federal government took back almost six million acres of this land. The government restricted the tribe to a reservation in Idaho that was one-tenth the size of their prior reservation. Joseph the Elder, feeling betrayed, destroyed his Bible and American flag, and refused to move from the Nez Perce homeland or to sign the treaty that would have made the new boundaries official.

Chief Joseph, who was designated Chief upon Joseph the Elder's death in 1871, inherited this volatile situation. In 1873, a federal order had seemed likely to remove white settlers and to let the Nez Perce remain, which would have calmed the situation. But the federal government reversed itself and fighting broke out between the Nez Perce and U.S. troops; the year was 1877. Joseph's warriors won several battles, but he realized they could not defeat the Army, led by General Howard. Chief Joseph ordered a retreat of the Nez Perce to Canada. He conducted the retreat so skillfully that he has been called the "Indian Napoleon." Even the U.S. Army was impressed with the 1,400-mile march. The retreat ended with Chief Joseph surrendering just miles from the Canadian border. Following is Chief Joseph's well-known 1877 speech, when he surrendered in the Bear Paw Mountains.

" I am tired of fighting. Our chiefs are killed. Looking Glass is dead. Toohoolhoolzote is dead. The old men are all dead. It is the young men who say, Yes or No. He who led the young men (Olikut) is dead. It is cold, and we have no blankets. The little children are freezing to death. My people, some of them, have run away to the hills, and have no blankets, no food. No one knows where they are – perhaps freezing to death. I want to have time to look for my children, and see how many of them I can find. Maybe I shall find them among the dead. Hear me, my chiefs! I am tired. My heart is sick and sad. From where the sun now stands I will fight no more forever".

Questions: Chief Joseph

1. **The Nez Perce originally lived in what valley?**
   Answer: *Wallowa Valley*
   Objectives/Expectations: *details; map skills; geography*

2. **Where is this valley located?**
   Answer: *Where Idaho, Oregon and Washington meet.*
   Objectives/Expectations: *explain how natural resources, resource needs, different perspectives, and trade relationships produce conflict and/or cooperation; geography, longitude/latitude*

3. **Nez Perce is French and means what?**
   Answer: *Pierced nose.*
   Objectives/Expectations: *vocabulary; culture; tradition*

4. **What does Hin-mah-too-yah-lat-kekt mean?**
   Answer: *Thunder Rolling Down the Mountains.*
   Objectives/Expectations: *vocabulary; culture; tradition*

5. **Who is the most well known of the Nez Perce Indians?**
   Answer: *Chief Joseph.*
   Objectives/Expectations: *examine how human and physical geography influence past decisions and events; feelings and emotions of characters; main idea*

6. **Explain in what way Chief Joseph's father cooperated with the territorial governor of Washington.**
   Answer: *Joseph the Elder helped the territorial governor set up a Nez Perce reservation.*
   Objectives/Expectations: *concerning geography ... identify where things (people, places, landmarks) are, how they are arranged, and why they are in particular locations; relationships*

7. **Describe what event took place to cause white settlers to move onto the Indian land.**

Answer: *Gold was found on the land.*

Objectives/Expectations: *evaluate past, current, and future issues of land use (preservation, development, modification) from geographic perspectives; sequential order; cause/effect*

8. **What did the U.S. government do after gold was found on the land?**

Answer: *The government took back 6 million acres of the Indian land. What then did Joseph the Elder do to evidence his feeling of betrayal?*

Objectives/Expectations: *explain how human and physical geography influence past decisions and events; examine essential roles of government in early cultures*

9. **What did Chief Joseph do after the U.S. government took back the Indian land?**

Answer: *He destroyed his Bible and American flag.*

Objectives/Expectations: *analyze conflicts on historical events and changes; explore ways in which belief systems, knowledge, and behavioral patterns define cultures and help to explain historical perspectives and events*

10. **In what year did fighting break out between the Nez Perce and the government?**

Answer: *In 1877.*

Objectives/Expectations: *detail to support main idea; dates, math concepts; prediction; outcome; relationships*

11. **Realizing he could not win the war, what did Chief Joseph decide to do?**

Answer: *He decided the tribe would retreat to Canada.*

Objectives/Expectations: *evaluate the interaction of humans with their environments; recognize the importance of physical environments — natural resources, etc.; understand the concept of scarcity; cause/effect; predict outcome*

12. **About how many miles did the tribe march?**

Answer: *About 1400.*

Objectives/Expectations: *use the five themes of geography (location, place, regions, movement, and relationships within places); relationships; cause/effect; predict outcome; logical conclusion; feelings and emotions; charts and graphs; measurement; map skills*

13. **Where did Chief Joseph surrender?**

Answer: *The Bear Paw Mountains.*

Objectives/Expectations: *geography; culture; feelings and relationships; outcome*

14. **Quote the famous last line from Chief Joseph's speech when he surrendered.**

Answer: *"From where the sun now stands I will fight no more forever".*

Objectives/Expectations: *author's purpose; feelings and emotions; analyze how governments reflect and impact culture; relationships*

1. Accounting is the language of business. It is important that anyone in the business world know enough of this "language" to be conversant with its terms.

2. Accounting is defined as the analyzing, classifying, recording, summarizing, and interpreting of business transactions in financial terms.

3. The fundamental accounting equation is this:

<u>Assets</u>	=	<u>Liabilities</u>	+	<u>Net Worth</u>
Items owned		Amounts owed		Owner's investment

The total of one side of the equation must always equal the total of the other side of the equation. If the equation is not in balance, an error has been made in the accounting process.

4. The next important concept to understand is the Chart of Accounts. This is the official list of accounts to be used in the books and financial statements of the business. There are different categories of accounts – they are listed below:

   Assets
   Liabilities
   Net Worth (also called Capital or Equity)
   Revenue
   Expenses

5. Examples of a few of the different kinds of accounts within each category might be:

<u>Assets</u>	<u>Liabilities</u>	<u>Net Worth</u>	<u>Revenue</u>	<u>Expenses</u>
Cash	Accounts payable	Stock	Sales	Wages
Accounts receivable	Taxes payable	Paid-in capital	Interest income	Rent
Equipment	Notes payable	Earnings	Miscellaneous income	Taxes

6. In order to record a financial transaction it is necessary to understand the concept of debits and credits. People often have a preconceived idea of what debit or credit means. But, simply, <u>debit means left and credit means right</u>. Each kind of account has a normal balance. And, each kind of account balance is **increased** in accordance with the graphic below:

<u>Assets</u>	=	<u>Liabilities</u>	+	<u>Net Worth</u>
Debit		Credit		Credit

These are also the normal account balances of these accounts.

Revenue and Expenses come under the "umbrella" of Net Worth. This is because at the end of the accounting cycle (usually 1 year), the Revenue and Expense accounts are netted and the resulting profit or loss goes in the Net Worth account. The graphic below shows how the balances in these accounts are **increased.**

<u>Revenue</u>   <u>Expenses</u>
Credit   Debit

These are also the normal account balances of these accounts.

7. Since Revenues and Expenses eventually become part of Net Worth, we can express the fundamental accounting equation this way also:

Assets   =   Liabilities   +   Net Worth

Owner's Investment + Revenues – Expenses

And also like this:

Assets   =   Liabilities   +   Net Worth   +   Revenue   –   Expenses

8. Accountants use "T-accounts" to show, in a simple way, how different accounts would appear when financial transactions are posted to them. We can also use these T-accounts to recap how each account is increased or decreased; that is, by debit or credit. It is essential to understand this concept before proceeding to actual entry of financial transactions. Learn this to the point of memorization so it becomes automatic in your thinking.

Assets =		Liabilities +		Net Worth +		Revenue –		Expense	
+	–	–	+	–	+	–	+	+	–
Debit	Credit	Debit	Credit	Debit	Credit	Debit	Credit	Debit	Credit

This information can be recapped like this:

To increase an Asset Account—debit the account.
To increase a Liability Account—credit the account.
To increase Net Worth—credit the account.
To increase a Revenue Account—credit the account.
To increase an Expense Account—debit the account.

9. Remember that the accounting equation must always balance. This means that debits and credits must be equal in each financial transaction that is recorded.

10. Whether the accounting process takes place manually or on computer, all the basic principles remain the same.

Questions: Introduction to Accounting

1. **Accounting is the ____________ of business.**
   Answer: *language*
   Objectives/Expectations: *word meaning; main idea*

2. **List all of the ways accountants deal with financial data.**
   Answer: *Accountants analyze, classify, record, summarize, and interpret financial data.*
   Objectives/Expectations: *main idea; summarization; definition and explanation; continue to develop number sense including fractions, decimals, and percents*

3. **Write the fundamental accounting equation.**
   Answer: *Assets = Liabilities + Net Worth*
   Objectives/Expectations: *relationships; math concepts; investigate and be able to use charts and graphs; show relationships between numbers and operations*

4. **What is the Chart of Accounts?**
   Answer: *The official list of accounts to be used in the books and financial statements.*
   Objectives/Expectations: *vocabulary; definition and explanation; understanding charts and graphs*

5. **What categories of accounts will be found in the Chart of Accounts?**
   Answer: *Assets, Liabilities, Net Worth, Revenue, and Expenses.*
   Objectives/Expectations: *supporting details; listing; vocabulary; charts and graphs; compare and contrast; reasonableness*

6. **What other names are used for Net Worth?**
   Answer: *Capital or Equity*
   Objectives/Expectations: *vocabulary; related details*

7. **Define debit; define credit.**
   Answer: *Debit means left; credit means right.*
   Objectives/Expectations: *vocabulary; determine the meanings of specialized terms; understanding charts and graphs; show relationships between numbers*

8. **Tell what the normal balance is for Assets, Liabilities, Net Worth, Revenue, and Expenses.**
   Answer: *Assets – debit; Liabilities – credit; Net Worth – credit; Revenue – credit; Expenses – debit.*
   Objectives/Expectations: *relationships; definition and explanation; extend understanding of operations; explain and apply properties*

9. **The net amount of Revenue and Expenses (i.e., profit or loss) will be put into which account at the end of the accounting cycle?**
   Answer: *Net Worth.*

Objectives/Expectations: *relationships; recognize economic concepts; make judgments; problem solving; collect, organize, and display data*

10. **Write the expanded fundamental accounting equation.**

Answer: *Assets = Liabilities + Net Worth + Revenue − Expenses*

Objectives/Expectations: *recognize economic concepts; relationships; solve problems with basic operations; reasonableness of solution*

11. **Explain the purpose of T-accounts.**

Answer: *T-accounts are used to show how various accounts would look after transactions are posted to them. It is a simple means of thinking about and "viewing" account activity.*

Objectives/Expectations: *inference; logical reasoning; draw conclusions; understanding and using charts and graphs; sequential ordering; organization; classification*

12. **In order for the accounting equation to balance, what must always be equal in every transaction?**

Answer: *Debits and credits must be equal.*

Objectives/Expectations: *relationships; number concepts; problem solving*

13. **True or false? With a good computerized accounting system it is not necessary to understand the fundamentals of accounting.**

Answer: *False.*

Objectives/Expectations: *inference; logical conclusion; critical thinking*

14. **Draw and label 5 T-accounts, one for each category of accounts. Then post the transactions below to the T–accounts.**

(1) The Rockrimmon Bed & Breakfast had income for the month of $5100, all paid in cash.

(2) The business borrowed $12,000 for improvements.

(3) The owners made a $255 monthly note payment. $155 was principal; $100 was interest.

(4) Wages were paid of $1800.

Answer:

Assets		Liabilities		Net Worth		Revenue		Expense	
(1) 5100							(1) 5100		
(2) 12000			(2) 12000						
	(3) 255	(3) 155						(3) 100	
	(4) 1800							(4) 1800	

Objectives/Expectations: *analysis; critical thinking; logical reasoning; sequential order; think and solve problems; solve problems with basic operations; understanding charts and graphs*

Look It Up!™

15. Complete the following sentences:

To increase an Asset, ___________ the account.
To increase a Liability, _________ the account.
To increase Net Worth, _________ the account.
To increase Revenue, __________ the account.
To increase an Expense, _______ the account.

Answer: *Asset – debit; Liability – credit; Net Worth – credit; Revenue – credit; Expense - debit.*

Objectives/Expectations: *recognize economic concepts; cause/effect relationships; problem-solving; model and formulate problems based on real-world situations*

16. If the Assets of a business are $1,500,000 and the Liabilities are $1,200,000, what is the amount of Net Worth?

Answer: *$300,000*

Objectives/Expectations: *analysis; relationships; critical thinking; logical reasoning; use basic operations, e.g., subtraction*

17. If the Net Worth of a business is $750,000 and the Liabilities are $200,000, how much are the Assets?

Answer: *$950,000.*

Objectives/Expectations: *analysis; relationships; critical thinking; logical reasoning; use addition; practice economic concepts and theories*

18. Complete the following sentences:

To decrease an Asset, _____________ the account.
To decrease a Liability, ___________ the account.
To decrease Net Worth, __________ the account.
To decrease Revenue, _____________ the account.
To decrease Expenses, ___________ the account.

Answer: *Asset – credit; Liability – debit; Net Worth – debit; Revenue – debit; Expenses –Credit.*

Objectives/Expectations: *analysis; logical conclusion; relationships; critical thinking; inference; problem solving; formulate problems based on real-world situations.*

Decimal Basics—Look It Up!™ Math

1. First, it's important to understand decimal place-value. Look at the numbers below.

0	. 4	5	8	9
ones	tenths	hundredths	thousandths	ten-thousandths

This number is read: "four thousand, five hundred eighty-nine ten-thousandths."

2. The places to the right of the decimal point are decimal places.
Practice listening to and reading other numbers:

    0.9   =   nine tenths

    0.23   =   twenty-three one hundredths

    0.752   =   seven hundred fifty-two thousandths

3. Often decimals are read and said another way. You can read 0.4589 as "point four five eight nine." The number 10.236 can be read as "ten and two hundred thirty-six thousandths," or as "ten point two three six."

4. It is important to know how to multiply decimals. First is an example of multiplying a whole number by a decimal.

```
   $1.45
 x   23
 ------
   4 35
  29 0
 ------
 $33.35
```

Notice that there are the same number of decimal places in the product as in the decimal factor ($1.45). Whenever a decimal is multiplied by a whole number, the product will have the same number of decimal places as the decimal factor.

5. When a decimal is multiplied by a decimal, the product has the same number of decimal places as the total number of decimal places in both factors.

```
    5.697
 x   4.11
    5697
    5697
  22788
 --------
 23.41467
```

Notice that the numbers 5.697 and 4.11 have a total of 5 decimal places. Notice that the product of the two numbers also has five decimal places. You multiply without worrying about the decimals; then after you have calculated the product, count five places from the right and place the decimal point.

6. It is easy to multiply decimals by 10, 100, or 1000. All you have to do is move the decimal point. Look at these examples.

10 x 9.651 = 96.51
When multiplying a decimal by 10, move the decimal point one place to the right.

100 x 9.651 = 965.1
When multiplying a decimal by 100, move the decimal point two places to the right.

1000 x 9.651 = 9651
When multiplying a decimal by 1000, move the decimal point three places to the right.

7. Dividing decimals by whole numbers is simple. The decimal point in the quotient is placed above the decimal point in the dividend. Look at the example below.

$$12 \overline{)\ 48.000}^{\ \ 4.000}$$ Notice how the decimal point is lined up.

8. Dividing decimals by 10, 100, or 1000 is not hard. Simply move the decimal point. Look at these examples.

673.4 ÷ 10 = 67.34
When dividing a *decimal* by 10, move its *decimal* point one place to the left.

673.4 ÷ 100 = 6.734
When dividing a *decimal* by 100, move its *decimal* point two places to the left.

673.4 ÷ 1000 = 0.6734
When dividing a *decimal* by 1000, move its *decimal* point three places to the left.

9. Often you will be asked to round a *decimal*. You will be asked to round to the nearest tenth, one-hundredth, or one-thousandth. Below are examples of rounding.

To the nearest tenth: 25.6915 would round to 25.7

To the nearest one-hundredth: 25.6915 would round to 25.69

To the nearest one-thousandth: 25.6915 would round to 25.692

1. In the spaces below, name the place-value.

______ . ______   ______   ______   ______

Answer:

ones . _tenths_   _hundredths_   _thousandths_   _ten-thousandths_

Objectives/Expectations: _place value; compare and contrast; greater than/less than_

2. What is another way to read decimals instead of saying "one and two hundred thirty-nine thousandths" for the number 1.239?

Answer: _It can be said as "one, point two three nine."_

Objectives/Expectations: _vocabulary; place-value; read, write and identify decimals through one-thousandths_

3. When multiplying a decimal by a whole number, how many decimal places will be in the product?

Answer: _The same number of decimal places as in the decimal factor will be in the product._

Objectives/Expectations: _whole numbers and decimals; number operations; place-value; understand and apply computational procedures_

4. When a decimal is multiplied by a decimal, how many decimal places will be in the product?

Answer: _The product will have the same number of decimal places as the total number of decimal places in both factors._

Objectives/Expectations: _mathematical terminology; place-value; number operations, e.g., multiplication_

5. Explain how to multiply a decimal by 10. By 100. By 1000.

Answer: _By 10— move the decimal point 1 place to the right._
            By 100—move the decimal point 2 places to the right.
            By 1000—move the decimal point 3 places to the right.

Objectives/Expectations: _number operations; place-value; explore estimation procedures; reasonableness of solution; logical deduction_

6. When dividing a decimal by a whole number, place the decimal _________ the decimal point in the dividend.

Answer: _above_

Objectives/Expectations: _applying number operations, whole numbers, and decimals, e.g., division; sequential order; follow directions and steps to reach correct conclusion; compare and order; and convert between whole numbers, fractions, and decimals_

7. **Explain how to divide decimals by 10. By 100. By 1000.**

Answer: *By 10—move the decimal point 1 place to the left.*

By 100—move the decimal point 2 places to the left

By 1000—move the decimal point 3 places to the left

Objectives/Expectations: *follow written directions; place-value; logical deduction; extend understanding of basic operations, whole numbers, fractions, and decimals*

8. **State the general principle of rounding numbers, that applies to decimals as well as to whole numbers.**

Answer: *Numbers below 5 are rounded down to the next lowest number, and numbers of 5 or greater are rounded up to the next highest number.*

Objectives/Expectations: *rounding and estimation; knowledge of basic number operations; place-value*

Elementary Mathematics—Look It Up!™ Math

Tell how many there are: Learning to count from 0 to 10. _______________

There is 1 square.

There are 2 triangles.

There are 3 circles.

There are 4 rectangles.

There are 5 cubes.

There are 6 happy faces.

There are 7 hearts.

There are 8 suns.

There are 9 moons.

There are 10 stars.

Here are the numbers from 1 to 10 in order:

1   2   3   4   5   6   7   8   9   10

The numbers can be spelled out, too:

ONE	TWO	THREE	FOUR	FIVE
SIX	SEVEN	EIGHT	NINE	TEN

Zero (0) is a special number; it means you don't have any. If you had 1 piece of candy and you ate it, you would have 0 pieces of candy.

0   ZERO

Working with numbers

When you count, the number that comes after another number is always 1 more. Look at the picture of the circles. If you draw 4 circles, then draw 1 more, you will have 5 circles.

4 circles   plus   one circle   equals   5 circles

When you count, the number that comes before another number is always 1 less. Look at the picture of the squares. If you draw 3 squares, then erase 1 square, you will have 2 squares.

3 squares   minus   1 square   equals   2 squares

To figure out what is 1 less, you can count backward. You count backward from 10 to 0 like this:

10   9   8   7   6   5   4   3   2   1

Signs we use when working with numbers: _______________________________________

This is the plus sign   **+**
We use the plus sign when we are adding numbers. For example: 1 + 1 = 2

This is the minus sign   **-**
We use the minus sign when we are subtracting numbers. For example: 2 – 1 = 1

This is the equals sign   **=**
We use the equals sign to show something is "the same as". For example:

2 + 1 = 3   Two plus one equals 3. Two plus one is the same as three.

Two boxes   plus   one box   equals   three boxes.
2 boxes   plus   1 box   equals   3 boxes.

Questions: Elementary Math

1.   ___T   ___F   A square has 4 sides, all of which are the same length.
     Answer: *True*
     Objectives/Expectations: *identify, describe, and make geometric figures; following written
                 directions*

2.   Rectangles have two sides that are the same _________ and two other sides that are the same
     length. Two of the sides are longer than the other two. This is a rectangle —
     Answer: *length*
     Objectives/Expectations: *compare and contrast; describe geometric figures; identify and draw
                 parallel lines*

3.   **Fill in the blank with the right answer. The numbers 1, 2, 3, 4, 5, 6, 7, 8, 9, and 10 can be
     spelled out. They are:**
     Answer: *(1) one (2) two (3) three (4) four (5) five (6) six (7) seven (8) eight (9) nine (10) ten*
     Objectives/Expectations: *number concepts; number-ordering; numerical and written numbers*

4. **Match the correct statements to the terms.**

1. When you are counting, the number that comes after another number is always 1 more. For example, five is one more than four. This is called:

   _2_ subtraction

2. (-) is a minus sign and is used in:

   _3_ equal

3. When numbers are added or subtracted to get answers that are the same, it is said that the numbers are:

   _1_ addition

Objectives/Expectations: *number operations; specialized terms; logical conclusion; problem-solving; prediction*

5. **Zero (0) is a special number – it means you don't have any. Give an example of when you would have zero as an answer.**

Answer: *If you ate the only piece of candy you had, then you would have zero pieces of candy.*

Objectives/Expectations: *follow written directions; determine word meanings; read, write, and count whole numbers*

6. **List the numbers that are missing in this number line: 1, 2, __, 4, 5, 6, __, __, 9, __**

Answer: *3, 7, 8, 10*

Objectives/Expectations: *number-ordering; following written directions*

7. **Which of the following groups of numbers have answers that are equal?**
(a) 4 + 4 = 8   5 + 3 = 8   (b) 3 + 4 = 7   6 + 2 = 8   (c) 1 + 4 = 5   2 + 5 = 7

Answer: *(a)*

Objectives/Expectations: *compare and contrast; number operations (addition); understand the meaning of "equal" and "unequal"*

8. **Which of the following numbers are not in order? 1, 2, 4, 5, 6, 7, 3, 8, 9, 10**

Answer: *3*

Objectives/Expectations: *read, write, and count whole numbers 0 – 10; compare and order numbers 1 through 10*

9. **Which sign matches the correct problem and answer? + (plus) or - (minus)**

		Answer:		
________	6 ___ 2 = 8		*(plus)*	*6 + 2 = 8*
________	7 ___ 2 = 5		*(minus)*	*7 - 2 = 5*
________	5 ___ 2 = 7		*(plus)*	*5 + 2 = 7*
________	3 ___ 3 = 0		*(minus)*	*3 - 3 = 0*

Objectives/Expectations: *use the basic operations of addition and subtraction; reasonableness of solution; problem-solving*

10. **Write sentences that tell what signs are used in addition, subtraction, and when numbers are equal.**

Look It Up!™

Answer: *When you are adding you use a plus (+) sign, and when you are doing subtraction, you use a minus (-) sign. When numbers are equal, you use an equal sign that looks like this (=).*

Objectives/Expectations: *following written directions; number operations; critical thinking; decision-making; reasonableness*

The Muscular System—Look It Up!™ Health

1. The muscular system is what makes your body move. There are various types of muscles; some move your inner organs and some move your skeleton. An example of muscle tissue that moves an inner organ is your heart muscle – this muscle keeps your heart beating. Another example of muscle tissue that moves organs is the stomach muscle – this muscle helps your food digest.

2. Most muscles are ***skeletal muscles***. They make you move when you walk, run, sit, stand, jump, lift something, wave to a friend, bend over, and when you talk. The skeletal muscles are attached to your skeleton either directly or by tendons. These muscles work in pairs. The *flexor* muscles bend joints when they contract. The *extensor* muscles straighten out joints. The skeletal muscles are *voluntary muscles* because you can control their movement. The cells of skeletal muscles are called *fibers* because they are long and threadlike. The fibers are *striated*, meaning they have crosswise stripes.

3. The muscles of the stomach and intestines are examples of ***smooth muscles***. Smooth muscles contract more slowly and rhythmically than skeletal muscles. In the case of stomach and intestinal muscles they contract to move food along for digestion. Blood vessels also have smooth muscles. The smooth muscles in blood vessels contract to make them narrow, or relax to make them wide. Smooth muscles cannot be controlled voluntarily, hence they are also called *involuntary muscles*. These muscles are not striped (striated) in appearance when you examine them under a microscope the way skeletal muscles are.

4. The ***cardiac muscle*** is the muscle tissue found only in the heart. It has striations like skeletal muscles, but it cannot be controlled voluntarily.

5. Skeletal muscles are stimulated by nerves. Smooth muscles are stimulated by a special set of nerves that belong to the *autonomic nervous system*, and by certain body chemicals called *hormones*. The autonomic nervous system regulates automatic bodily processes such as digestion.

6. Any well-made machine may, in time, develop a problem. The same is true of the muscular system. The kinds of problems that can develop include *muscle tears* and *muscle strains*. Muscle tears occur when the muscle fibers are separated by sudden force – such as kicking a ball too hard. Muscle strain happens when a muscle is overused. For example, you could feel muscle strain on the first day of football practice. Muscle strain is less serious than a muscle tear.

Questions: The Muscular System

1. Name the 3 main types of muscles.

   Answer: *Skeletal, smooth, and cardiac.*

   Objectives/Expectations: *main idea; details; examine interdependencies of organs*

2. What does it mean when we say a muscle is a voluntary muscle?
   Give an example of this muscle group.

   Answer: *It means we can control the movement of it. Skeletal muscles are voluntary.*

   Objectives/Expectations: *following written directions; understanding specialized terms; investigate behavioral responses to internal changes and external stimuli*

3. What does it mean when we say a muscle is involuntary?
   Give an example of this muscle group.

   Answer: *We cannot control the movement of these muscles. An example of this group is the stomach muscle.*

   Objectives/Expectations: *vocabulary; context clues; analyze science as it relates to everyday life*

4. True or false – extensor muscles bend joints when they contract.

   Answer: *False*

   Objectives/Expectations: *context clues; determine meaning of unfamiliar words; investigate internal responses*

5. True or false – cardiac muscle is found only in the heart.

   Answer: *True*

   Objectives/Expectations: *details; interactions between organs*

6. Describe how skeletal muscles and smooth muscles are stimulated.

   Answer: *Skeletal muscles are stimulated by nerves. Smooth muscles are stimulated by special nerves in the autonomic nervous system, and by hormones.*

   Objectives/Expectations: *investigate behavioral responses to internal changes and external stimuli; examine factors that influence the interactions between organs*

7. Which of the muscles does not have stripes or striations?

   Answer: *Smooth muscles.*

   Objectives/Expectations: *compare and contrast; vocabulary; multi-meaning words*

8. Name the 2 common types of problems that can develop in the muscular system.

   Answer: *The 2 kinds of problems that can occur are muscle strains and muscle tears.*

   Objectives/Expectations: *sequential order; making judgments; behavioral responses to external stimuli*

Look It Up!™

Look It Up!™ Simplified Instructions for Use with Worksheets

1. The teacher puts students into groups of 2, 3, or 4 per group.

2. Each student is given a copy of the same worksheet.

3. The teacher twice asks a question pertaining to the worksheet.

4. Students place their hands on their worksheet. When the teacher says, "Go," the students may begin to locate the answer and/or solve a problem to get the answer.

5. The first group teacher to raise his/her hand (after all members of the group know the answer) is called on and asked the location of the answer.

6. If the location is correct, the teacher says, "Go ahead."

7. If the location is incorrect, the teacher says, "Thank you very much," and calls on another group to answer.

8. When the location is correct, the teacher may call on any group member to explain the answer.

9. If the explanation is unsatisfactory, the teacher says, "Thank you very much," and calls on another group to answer.

10. The group whose member answers correctly and offers an understandable explanation, may say where the hands are placed while the next question is asked.

11. The game continues the same as in rules 3 through 10.

Math Look It Up!™ Worksheet Example

Understanding the reasonableness of solution strategies, problem-solving, and analysis.

Use worksheets to help students reason, draw, calculate, use self-talk; and to think about what problems are asking, what operations are needed, how to think through problems, work problems to arrive at correct conclusions, and proof their work. Look It Up!™ can be used with basic elementary math, geometry, problem-solving, virtually any operation or instruction in any text. It helps students communicate, make connections, reason, apply knowledge, and extend thinking skills.

Rounding and Estimation ____

1. 92 people traveled to Carol's farm by car; 49 people went there by bus. About how many more people went by car? Mark your answer.
   A. 150   B. 50   C. 40   D. 30

2. Mark saw 29 birds and 42 fish at the zoo. About how many animals did he see at the zoo? Mark your answer.
   A. 110   B. 100   C. 70   D. 30

3. Gabriel rode 38 rides on vacation. Lori rode 41 rides. Which would be the best way to find about how many rides they rode altogether? Mark your answer.
   A. 40 + 40   B. 30 + 40   C. 20 + 30   D. 40 + 50

4. Tanisha saved $120 for a new winter coat. The coat cost $98 with tax. About how much money did she have after she bought the coat? Mark your answer.
   A. Less than $20   B.   Between $10 and $40
   C. Between $50 and $100   D.   More than $100

5. Sarah picked 47 flowers. Maria picked 16 flowers. About how many more flowers did Sarah pick than Maria? Mark your answer.
   A. 30   B.   40
   C. 50   D.   70

6. Sue bought a pack of gum for 33¢. She had 50¢ to pay for it. About how much change would she get back? Mark your answer.
   A. 80¢   B.   60¢
   C. 40¢   D.   20¢

Look It Up!™ Questions for Worksheet – Rounding & Estimating to the Nearest 10 and 100

1. In problem 2, what word tells you to add 29 and 42? What is the answer? Why did you round and estimate to that number?
   Answer: *"and"; C-70; 71 is rounded down to 70 because 71 is closer to 70 than 80.*

2. In problem 4, how much money did Tanisha have left? Why is "A" not the answer? What is the answer?
   Answer: *$22; "A" can't be the answer because "A" says "less than $20"; B – between $10 and $40.*

3. What words in problem 6 tell you to subtract to get the answer? What is the answer? Why did you round up rather than down?

Answer: *How much change would she get back?; $ .17; round to 20 because 17 is closer to 20*
                      than to 10, and 17 is more than 15.

4. Why did you subtract in problem 5? What is the answer? Why did you round down?

Answer: *Because the problem asked "... how many more flowers did Sarah pick than Maria?";*
                      A-30 (31); 31 rounds down to 30.

5. In problem 1, how did you know the answer wasn't A – 150? What is the answer? Did you round up or down to get the answer?

Answer: *Because the question was, "About how many more people went by car?" so you would have*
                      to subtract instead of add; 40 [43]; round down.

6. What did you have to think to get the answer in problem 3?

Answer: *Since they asked, "how many rides they rode altogether," and you would round 38 to 40*
                      and 41 to 40, the answer would be A—40 + 40.

Primary/Elementary Math Look It Up!™ Worksheet Example

Understanding number concepts, addition, subtraction, multiplication, or division to solve problems
Determining solution strategies and problem-solving

Examples of how carelessness, lack of following directions, and misunderstanding lead to failure:

(1) X X x x   X X x X X   X X x

(2) X X   x x X   X x   x X X

(3) x x X   x x x X   X X X

(4) X x x x x X   X X x X

(5) X x X x   X X x X

(6) X   X x x x X x X x x X

1. Which line shows 4 + 4?
    Answer: *Line 5*

2. Which line does not have an even number as its total?
    Answer: *Line 6*

3. Which line shows the greater sum, line 3 or line 5?
    Answer: *Line 3*

4. How many small x's are in lines 4 and 6?
    Answer: *5 in Line 4 and 6 in Line 6*

5. What is the difference in small x's in lines 2 and 5?
    Answer: *1 (4 - 3 = 1)*

More Difficult Math—Look It Up!™ Worksheet Example

Understanding the reasonableness of solution strategies, problem-solving, and analysis

1. The price of a bus fare from Denver to Colorado Springs increased by 60% over a one–year period. To find the amount of increase in a ticket originally priced at $85, multiply $85 by 1/60; 3/50; 1/6; 3/5. Explain your reasoning.

   Work Space:

   Answer: *3/5 – re-wrote 60% as a fraction 60/100 and reduced*

2. $3 \cdot (6 + 2) =$ (a) $3 \cdot 6 + 3 \cdot 2$ (c) $3 \cdot 6 + 2$
                    (b) $(3 + 6) \cdot 2$ (d) $(3 + 6) \cdot (3 + 2)$

   Explain your reasoning.

   Work Space:

   $3 \cdot (6 + 2) = 3 \cdot 8$ added inside the parentheses first   (Example)
   $3 \cdot 8 = 24$ multiplied next
   $3 \cdot 6 + 3 \cdot 2 = 18 + 6$ multiplied first
   $18 + 6 = 24$ added next

   Since the answer was the same for both expressions, $3 \cdot (6 + 2) = 3 \cdot 6 + 3 \cdot 2$
   Answer: *(a) $3 \cdot 6 + 3 \cdot 2$*

3. Mr. Hill decided to get more exercise. He walked 2.5 miles the first week, 3.75 miles the second week, 5 miles the third week, and 6.25 miles the fourth week. If the pattern continues, how many miles will Mr. Hill walk the seventh week? What is the pattern?
   (a) 10 miles (b) 11.25 miles (c) 15 miles   (d) 17.5 miles

   Work Space:

   Answer: *(a) 10 miles   He adds 1.25 miles a week*

4. Differentiate between the figures. Which has a right angle; which has an obtuse angle; and which has an acute angle? How many degrees are in: a right angle, an acute angle; and an obtuse angle?
   (a)   (b)   (c)

   Answer: *(a) is a right angle (b) is an acute angle (c) is an obtuse angle. A right angle has a measure of 90º. An acute angle measures less than 90º. An obtuse angle measures more than 90º but less than 180º.*

Look It Up!™

CHAPTER 3

Dots'n'Boxes™

OR

"One of the Reasons I Failed Church"

If you're old enough, you'll remember playing this game—probably at church. If you're too young to have played, it's never too late to learn. Almost every Sunday in church, during the sermon, my friends and I would sit in the balcony and draw rows of dots stacked on top of each other to make grids of dots on the backs of offering envelopes. Then we'd take turns drawing one line at a time, connecting two of the dots. When the line we made enclosed all the sides of a single box, we'd place our initials in the center of that box. When all the dots were connected to enclose all the boxes, and all the boxes were filled with initials, then the person with the most initialed boxes won the game. I'm sure there are games that are more fun, but not during church.

Anyway . . . we loved it. It got us through lots of sermons (and got me into hot water more times than I care to admit). Oh, but I'd get excited. When it got down to the wire and any more marks would close a box, we'd giggle, ooh and aah, and will ourselves to win. Sometimes I willed myself a little too loudly, a little too boisterously, and the preacher would look up into that balcony, shake his finger, shake his head and say, in his really, really deep voice, "Boys and girls, . . . This is the Lord's house." That would do it. My fate was sealed. Without even looking down on the main floor, I knew my Mama was sitting in that pew, hymnal in hand, fanning herself. I knew I had brought on another hot flash and was going to either get a spankin' or a talkin'-to when we got home. Even if I could recite all the books of the Bible, I had still failed church!

My religious shortcomings might have been the makings of newspaper headlines in Vernon, Texas. I suppose my Sunday School teachers deserved sainthood almost as much as my school teachers. A few weeks ago, I ran into a man who had been one of my Daddy's friends. He said he heard my voice and "just knew that voice belonged to Lauretta Lawrence." I'll bet I hadn't seen him in twenty years. He grinned and asked, "Lauretta, wasn't it you who 'rededicated your life' every time the invitation song was "Just As I Am?" Oh man! I'm over fifty and my youth still comes back to haunt me! "Yes," I said. "When they'd sing all the verses and start humming, I'd stand there waiting, being very quiet, being very good. I'd wait and wait, and wait, but they still kept humming. Until I went down to the front of the church, that is. I never knew exactly what I'd done wrong, but I'd go down the aisle, and once I got to the front, they'd stop the singing. I just knew it was me they were waiting for." Maybe it was playing Dots and Boxes in the balcony. Maybe it was using a compact mirror to reflect light to try to start a fire with the pages of my Sunday School book. I don't know. Whatever caused it, my mother said she quit counting the times I rededicated my life when the count reached sixty-seven. To this day, I still can't hear "Just As I Am" and "Amazing Grace" without feeling blessed and grateful, and a tinge remorseful about my behavior in church.

But Mama survived and so did I. And even now, just like in my younger days, I still mess up on occasion just like some of our kids. I still get blamed. But as I recall, our preachers came and went quite frequently. I really don't think it was all my fault. Even if it was . . . I'm not taking all the blame!

I will, however, take the blame for getting a little too exuberant with Dots and Boxes, Hangman, and Tic-Tac-Toe in the balcony of that First Baptist Church. Sometimes we listened to the sermon, sometimes we didn't. We were kids! But just think about it . . . if these little games can entertain thousands of kids on countless Sundays, they can most assuredly work in the classroom. We don't have to have fancy, expensive games or activities to pull kids into a lesson or review. Whatever entices kids to participate and become active, involved learners is all we need. S.M.A.R.T.S.™ Dots'n'Boxes™ does just that.

I started putting the Dots'n'Boxes™ game and score sheet together at least fifteen years ago. It has truly gone through a thorough evolution to get to where it is today. Just as in Look It Up,™ this chapter had to include both academic and behavioral objectives. On the score sheet itself, I wanted to track right and wrong answers, daily behavior, and individual involvement. I wanted the students to help each other with prompts, and to view giving help and receiving help as a good thing. As it is, the score sheet keeps track of these targets, yet is simple and easy to use. I guess the whole idea is fairly simple: give kids something they like, something that's a challenge, something that yields a winner . . . and you'll have one yourself. Use Dots'n'Boxes™ a lot, but use the stuff you come up with, too. You just never know!

S.M.A.R.T.S.™ Dots'n'Boxes™

S.M.A.R.T.S.™ Dots'n'Boxes™ helps behavior, vocabulary, listening, comprehension, retention and recall, retrieval, and social skills. Learning is made easier because clues from team members provide repetition and remediation. Students feel good about themselves when they answer a question correctly, as well as when they are designated helpers. Students learn it is okay to give and to receive help. Because of the structure of Dots'n'Boxes,™ the teacher is free to move about the room to monitor and provide immediate feedback. This strategy is used primarily for review, but it can also be effective when clues or hints cause something to click in the student's mind, encouraging recollection, logical deduction, analysis, and critical thinking.

Dots'n'Boxes,™ can be used with any subject content. It is an excellent tool for practicing skills such as reading comprehension, phonics, sequential order in math word problems, writing, science formulas, and math ordering. Use it to assist with prefixes and suffixes, parts of speech, dictionary and reference skills, math concepts and operations, health, social studies, geography, steps for following instructions to reach conclusions, music, art, various content facts, test preparation, classification, steps in drawing conclusions and predicting outcomes, logical reasoning, and problem solving. In essence, teachers can use this strategy to introduce daily objectives, concept or theme objectives, and anything teachers want to present for students to retain information and improve recall.

Instructions

1. The teacher presents informational or content material to the class using whatever method he/she chooses.

2. The teacher discusses that content with the class.

3. The teacher divides the class into teams, having no more than 6 members per team. If a student[s] needs to work paired with another student, the teacher should pair students in the class to avoid embarrassing anyone.

4. The teacher gives every team a Dots'n'Boxes™ score card, and a marking pen. *(Laminating the cards allows them to be used repeatedly. I also give each student a score card to mark individually.)*

5. Questions are written on paper, packets, or on note cards with the answers included. Questions may come from either the text or worksheets. Answers must be included.

6. Beginning with one person as the first Group Teacher, the teacher gives questions and answers or a question/answer packet to the Group Teacher (GT)—face down.

7. The person to the GT's left is the Questioned Student (QS).

8. The student to the QS's left is the First Group Helper (GH1). Each GH states clues so everyone can hear and participate. To the left of GH 1 is the Second Group Helper (GH2). To the left of the Group Helper is the Rules

Keeper/Time Keeper (RK/TK). If the team consists of only four players, the RK/TK also serves as the second Group Helper. If there are six persons on a team, the extra player becomes Group Helper 3.

9. The role of Group Teacher (GT), Questioned Student (QS), Group Helpers (GH), and Rules and Time Keeper (RK/TK) change after each question, with the jobs always rotating clockwise.

10. The teacher explains the procedures and rules of the activity, models the activity, plays a sample round consisting of one question with the students, and checks for understanding.

11. The first Group Teacher selects a question and shows the question and its answer to every person in the group except the person to his/her immediate left, who is the [QS] Questioned Student, the person who will be asked the question.

12. After all group members except the QS have seen the question and answer, the Group Teacher [GT] reads the question to the QS.

13. The QS has 20 seconds to respond and answer the question. If the answer is correct, the QS marks four lines, connecting dots on the score card to try to form a box.

14. In all cases, when a student marks a line (connects two dots) that encloses a box, that person may place his/her initials in the center of the box.

15. All other team members (GT, GH1, GH2, and RK/TK) who participate by performing their duties may connect two dots to create a single line, attempting to also complete a box on the score card.

16. If the QS is incorrect, the person to the immediate left of the QS (the first designated helper, Group Helper 1) offers the QS a one-word clue to help the QS arrive at the correct answer. All Group Helpers state their clues aloud so everyone can hear and participate. Younger students may offer complete sentences as clues rather than one- or two-word clues.

17. If the clue helps QS answer correctly, both QS and the helper may mark three lines in the box in an effort to complete closed boxes, with the QS marking first. Each of the other team members [who actively participate by performing their duties] marks one line on the score card.

18. If the QS again answers incorrectly, the person to the immediate left of the GH1, the Second Group Helper (GH2), offers a two-word clue for assistance. The clue is stated aloud so everyone can hear and participate. If this two-word clue elicits the correct response, the QS and both helpers mark two lines each, with the QS again marking first. Each remaining team member who actively participates by performing his/her duties marks one line.

19. If the QS once more answers incorrectly, the Group Teacher states the correct answer for the QS. Each group member explains his/her clue, and all team members connect two dots to make one line each, again in an attempt to create a closed box on the score card. No matter what, each clue-giver and the group teacher make one mark, as does the QS, as long as the person has made an effort to answer, offer clues, or perform duties. If a student has made no effort to be an active member of the game, the student is not allowed to mark a line.

20. This completes the first round. Now the duties of GT, QS, GH1, GH2, and RK/TK all rotate clockwise so that the QS becomes the Group Teacher; the person to his/her immediate left becomes the new QS; the next, the GH1 followed by the GH2 (also the RK/TK in a four-person team), and the first GT now becomes the RK/TK. The new GT asks the next question to begin Round 2.

21. The first team in the classroom to completely answer all the questions is declared the winning team. The person on each team with the most initialed boxes wins as well. Members of the winning team may practice writing test questions in their own words until all teams have finished the game. Other teams may write practice questions as they complete the game until the final team has finished. The teacher may award extra points for this effort, or the teacher may reward the students with "free reading" time following the completion of a game. Students may read anything they choose as long as the reading material is suitable and approved by the teacher.

Dots'n'Boxes™—Simplified Instructions

1. Students study the information.

2. Teacher assigns 4 to 6 people to a team and appoints a Group Teacher.

3. Group Teacher shows the question to the group so each member can be thinking of a one or two-word clue, with the exception of the Questioned Student on the left of the Group Teacher.

4. Group Teacher asks question two times.

5. Sequence of marking on the score card:

    a. If QS answers correctly, QS draws 4 marks. Each other team member performs his or her duty or states his/her one-word clue and draws one mark each. The GT draws one mark.

    b. If QS does not answer correctly, the person on left of QS (Group Helper 1) gives a one-word clue to QS. If clue helps QS answer correctly, QS and GH1 draw three marks each. All other team members perform duties or state their clues and draw one mark. GT draws one mark.

    c. If QS doesn't answer correctly after GH1's clue, Group Helper 2 gives the QS a two-word clue. If clue helps QS get answer, QS, GH1, and GH2 draw two marks each. Other team members perform duties or give one-word clues and draw one mark apiece. GT draws one mark.

    d. If QS answers incorrectly, team members continue giving one-word clues until QS answers correctly or until everyone has offered a one-word clue. In either case, all helpers draw one mark. The GT tells QS the answer if necessary and draws one mark, and QS draws a mark for trying. If QS doesn't try, he/she does not get to connect dots to make a mark.

6. The turn and the jobs of the players—not the players themselves—rotate to the left. The next question is asked by the new GT.

Dots'n'Boxes™ Scoring Summary

Person	Clues Received/Given	QS	Lines Drawn Helpers	Others
Questioned Student	No clues Needed	4		
Group Helpers, Group Teacher, and all students who gave clues and/or performed their jobs				1
Questioned Student	Received one clue—answer correct	3		
Group Helper	Gave 1 clue for correct answer		3	
All other team members who did their jobs or told what their clue would have been				1
Questioned Student	Received 2 clues—answer correct	2		
Group Helper 1	Gave 1 clue—answer incorrect		2	
Group Helper 2	Gave 1 clue—answer correct		2	
All other team members who offered clues and/or did their jobs				1
Questioned Student	Received additional clue(s)— eventually answered correctly	1		
Group Helper 1	Gave 1 clue—answer incorrect		1	
Group Helper 2	Gave 1 clue—answer incorrect		1	
All other team members who offered clues and/or did their jobs				1
Questioned Student	Received clues—did not answer question correctly but tried	1		
All other team members who offered clues and/or did their jobs				1
Anyone who did not perform his/her job as described, or attempt to answer or participate, including QS				0

Note: If Group Helper 1 gives a clue and Group Helper 2 says, "He/She Group Helper 1) gave my clue," then Group Helper 1 gets Group Helper 2's mark. No effort always yields no marks.

Dots'n'Boxes™ Score Sheet with Instructions

This sample Game/Score Sheet explains the scoring procedure—who draws lines to connect dots and what is considered to determine how many lines each student may draw during each round of play. The goal is to create enclosed boxes bounded by four lines. The student drawing the last line which closes off a box, places his or her initials inside that box. Once all boxes are enclosed, the student having the most initialed boxes wins the game.

Scoring Summary:

GT asks question two times:

QS answers question w/o help: _________________ QS draws four lines/1 mark each performing job/giving clue

QS answers question with help of
1 helper using one-word clue: __________ QS & GH1 draw three lines each/1 mark each doing jobs/giving clues

QS answers question with help of
2nd helper using two-word clue: _ QS, GH1 & GH2 draw two lines each/1 mark each doing jobs/giving clues

QS answers question with help of any
other team members using a one-word clue: ____________ QS & all GH offering clues/doing jobs/ 1 line each

GT tells QS the answer and QS tells which
clue would have helped the most: _________________ GT, QS, and all active participants draw 1 line each

Each team fills in the subject line, the class period, date, lesson, team number in the appropriate line on the Score Card. When the game is completed, the team averages itºs individual scores and circles the appropriate Team Score before handing in the Score Card.

SUBJECT: _______________________________ CLASS PERIOD: ____________ DATE: _________________

LESSON: ____________________ TEAM ________ TEAM SCORE: 100   90   80   70   60   50
            (Chapter/Unit/Review Topic)

TEAM MEMBERS		INDIVIDUAL SCORE				
Lauretta	100	90	80	70	60	50
Sandra	100	90	80	70	60	50
John	100	90	80	70	60	50
David	100	90	80	70	60	50

Each team member's name is listed in the space provided. The numbers to the right of the name reflect the individual participation score for the class time during which the game is played. Each student starts with a participation grade of 100. The only way a student may lose points is by: 1) not paying attention; 2) not following directions; and 3) disrupting class members. If students pay attention, are not disruptive, and follow directions, they are more inclined to learn. However, each time a team member incurs one of these infractions, a slash mark is made through one of the grades, starting with 100. When 10 points are removed from an individual student, the same amount is taken from the group as well since part of the group's goal is to work well together and support and encourage each other in the learning process. Once points are removed from a student's or the group's score, points may be re-added to the group's score (if they are truly trying to comply with all rules and discourage misbehavior), but points may not be re-added to an individual student's scores. Consequences are consequences, and students need to learn that we can't always act or talk our way out of a situation. If the lower participation score was earned, then that score will be received for that particular day. The next time Dots'n'Boxes™ is played, all students again start with the grade of 100, and it is theirs alone to keep or lose.

When students give correct answers, clues, or assistance (as per the instructions), they draw the pre-scribed number of lines between pairs of dots, attempting to create closed boxes. Remember that the number of lines depends on the answer, the number of clues, and group participation. Whenever a student draws a line which closes in a box on the grid, he/she places his/her initials in that box. The student with the most initialed boxes is the winner of that team. The team then hands in the Score Card to the teacher.

© 1996 Revised 2001 Lauretta Buchanan S.M.A.R.T.S.™ Learning System

Complete Dots'n'Boxes™ Score Sheets are found on pages 61 and 62. The Score Sheet on page 61 is used when students are learning the scoring rules. The Score Sheet on page 62 can be used after students have mastered the scoring rules. Two Practice Score Sheets are also included.

Dots'n'Boxes™ Practice Score Sheet

Scoring Summary:

GT asks question two times:

QS answers question w/o help: _______________ QS draws four lines/1 mark each performing job/giving clue

QS answers question with help of
1 helper using one-word clue: _________ QS & GH1 draw three lines each/1 mark each doing jobs/giving clues

QS answers question with help of
2nd helper using two-word clue: _ QS, GH1 & GH2 draw two lines each/1 mark each doing jobs/giving clues

QS answers question with help of any
other team members using a one-word clue: ___________ QS & all GH offering clues/doing jobs/ 1 line each

GT tells QS the answer and QS tells which
clue would have helped the most: _________________ GT, QS, and all active participants draw 1 line each

SUBJECT:_________________________ CLASS PERIOD: ___________ DATE: ______________

LESSON: ___________________ TEAM ________ TEAM SCORE: 100 90 80 70 60 50
(Chapter/Unit/Review Topic)

TEAM MEMBERS	INDIVIDUAL SCORE
_________________________________	100 90 80 70 60 50
_________________________________	100 90 80 70 60 50
_________________________________	100 90 80 70 60 50
_________________________________	100 90 80 70 60 50

Dots'n'Boxes™ Practice Score Sheet

Scoring Summary:

GT asks question two times:

QS answers question w/o help: _______________ QS draws four lines/1 mark each performing job/giving clue

QS answers question with help of
1 helper using one-word clue: _________ QS & GH1 draw three lines each/1 mark each doing jobs/giving clues

QS answers question with help of
2nd helper using two-word clue: _ QS, GH1 & GH2 draw two lines each/1 mark each doing jobs/giving clues

QS answers question with help of any
other team members using a one-word clue: ____________ QS & all GH offering clues/doing jobs/ 1 line each

GT tells QS the answer and QS tells which
clue would have helped the most: _________________ GT, QS, and all active participants draw 1 line each

SUBJECT: _____________________________ CLASS PERIOD: ____________ DATE: ________________

LESSON: ____________________ TEAM ________ TEAM SCORE: 100   90   80   70   60   50
      (Chapter/Unit/Review Topic)

TEAM MEMBERS   INDIVIDUAL SCORE

______________________________________   100   90   80   70   60   50

______________________________________   100   90   80   70   60   50

______________________________________   100   90   80   70   60   50

______________________________________   100   90   80   70   60   50

Dots'n'Boxes™ Score Sheet*

Scoring Summary:

GT asks question two times:

QS answers question w/o help: _________________ QS draws four lines/1 mark each performing job/giving clue

QS answers question with help of
1 helper using one-word clue: _________ QS & GH1 draw three lines each/1 mark each doing jobs/giving clues

QS answers question with help of
2nd helper using two-word clue: _ QS, GH1 & GH2 draw two lines each/1 mark each doing jobs/giving clues

QS answers question with help of any
other team members using a one-word clue: ___________ QS & all GH offering clues/doing jobs/ 1 line each

GT tells QS the answer and QS tells which
clue would have helped the most: _________________ GT, QS, and all active participants draw 1 line each

SUBJECT: _______________________________ CLASS PERIOD: _____________ DATE: __________________

LESSON: ____________________ TEAM _________ TEAM SCORE: 100   90   80   70   60   50
     (Chapter/Unit/Review Topic)

TEAM MEMBERS	INDIVIDUAL SCORE
_______________________________________	100 90 80 70 60 50
_______________________________________	100 90 80 70 60 50
_______________________________________	100 90 80 70 60 50
_______________________________________	100 90 80 70 60 50

Dots'n'Boxes™ Score Sheet*

SUBJECT: _________________________ CLASS PERIOD: _________ DATE: _____________

LESSON: _________________ TEAM _______ TEAM SCORE: 100   90   80   70   60   50
(Chapter/Unit/Review Topic)

TEAM MEMBERS	INDIVIDUAL SCORE

TEAM MEMBERS							
________________________________	100	90	80	70	60	50
________________________________	100	90	80	70	60	50
________________________________	100	90	80	70	60	50
________________________________	100	90	80	70	60	50
________________________________	100	90	80	70	60	50
________________________________	100	90	80	70	60	50
________________________________	100	90	80	70	60	50

© 1996 Revised 2001 Lauretta Buchanan S.M.A.R.T.S.™ Learning System

This page may be reproduced without permission for limited classroom use only . No other pages in this book may be reproduced without the express written consent of the publisher unless otherwise designated.

Dots'n'Boxes™ Rotation of Play Diagram

The first row in the following diagram demonstrates the setup, assignment of duties and rotation of play for Dots'n'Boxes™ for four, five or six players per team. The succeeding rows demonstrate the clockwise rotation of the duties for each successive Round. A Round consists of one question. Note that the duties pass from student to student in a clockwise rotation—**the students themselves do not move.** GT is the Group Teacher. QS is the Questioned Student. GH1, 2 and 3 are Group Helpers, and finally, RK/TK is the Rules and Time Keeper. Note that when there are only four players per team, the RK/TK also serves as Group Helper 2.

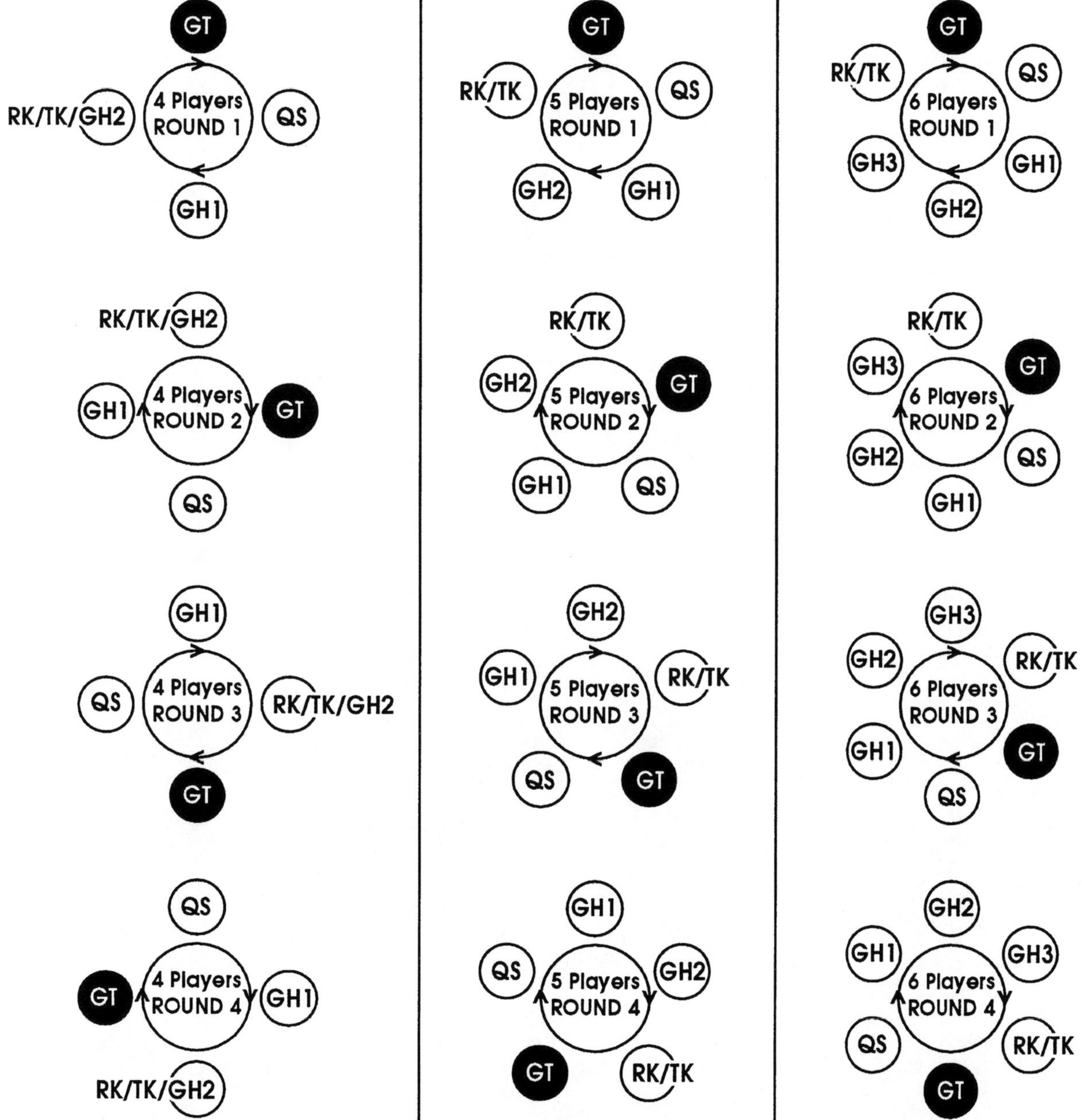

The Story of Honest Abe—Dots'n'Boxes™ U.S. History

1. Many people consider Abraham Lincoln to be one of our greatest presidents.

2. Abraham Lincoln was born on February 12, 1809, in Kentucky. When he was seven years old, his family moved to Indiana. It was a hard trip through the wilderness because there were no roads.

3. There is a story that Lincoln lived in Indiana for a while in a log cabin that had only three sides. The fourth side was open to the air. It had no door, no window, and no chimney. It did not even have a floor! After a while Lincoln and his father built a better cabin, but it was very plain and life was hard.

4. In Indiana, many of the schoolhouses were very poor. They had fireplaces to warm the children, but only dirt for floors. There was no glass for the windows. Strips of oiled paper were pasted across the openings instead. There were no desks. Logs were split in half for seats.

5. Books were very scarce in those days. Most people did not own any, except for a Bible. To do his arithmetic, Abraham used the back of a shovel for a slate to write on, and a burned stick of wood for a pencil. He would do his arithmetic and reading by the light of the fire.

6. A story is told of how, when Lincoln was young, he borrowed a book from a neighbor. The book was about George Washington. Abe read the book until it was time for bed. To keep it safe, he stuck it between two logs of the cabin. It rained and the book was soaked through.

7. The very next morning Abe took the book back to its owner and said that he had ruined the book. He then offered to pay for it. The man was happy because young Lincoln was so honest. From then on, Lincoln was known as "Honest Abe."

8. Young Lincoln never stopped learning, even though he had to quit school and get a job. He studied long and hard on his own and became a lawyer. Soon he was so well known for his honesty and his knowledge of law that he was elected to Congress. In 1860, Honest Abe was elected President.

Questions: The Story of Honest Abe

(Note: Suggestion for variation for *Dots'n'Boxes.*™ Students could play Dots'n'Boxes™ this way: (1) the clue giver gives his/her clue orally; (2) the QS answers out loud and the other team members write the answer on their worksheets as a question is answered correctly; (3) all team members make a mark on their Dots'n'Boxes™ Score Sheet according to the scoring rules. Clue givers may use the story to look up the correct answers for their clues.)

1. **Why was it hard for Abraham Lincoln's family to move from Kentucky to Indiana?**
    Answer: *The land was wilderness with no road.*

Objectives/Expectations: *details; cause/effect; inference & conclusion; setting; time; geography; understand surroundings; understand physical and human characteristics of places and regions; recognize factors that influence human movement and settlement*

2. **Compare the schoolhouses when Abraham Lincoln was a boy to schools of today. Which would have been more pleasant to attend? Why?**

   Answer: *The schoolhouses when Abraham Lincoln was a boy were different from our schools of today. Many, both then and today, are very poor, but they were built differently. Abraham Lincoln's school used a fireplace to warm the children and had a dirt floor. We use either individual room heaters and air conditioning units or have central heating and cooling. We also have concrete, wooden, brick or some other kind of floor, but our floors are not dirt. Our windows are made of glass, while they had strips of oiled paper pasted across the window opening. Lincoln's school had no desks and logs were split in half to make the seats. As a rule, we have desks with seats or tables with chairs.*

   Objectives/Expectations: *compare/contrast; cause/effect; setting; time; determine the meanings of specialized terms; details; follow written directions; summarization; generalization; draw conclusions; analyze information and make judgments; fact/nonfact; recognize economic concepts; recognize relationships among work, wages, purchasing power, and lifestyle*

3. **How did Abraham Lincoln get the nickname, "Honest Abe"?**

   Answer: *He had borrowed a book about George Washington from a neighbor. When he finished reading it for the night, he stuck it between two logs of the cabin to keep it safe. That night, it rained and the book was ruined. The very next morning Abe took the book back to the man and offered to pay for the book. The man was very impressed with Abraham Lincoln's honesty.*

   Objectives/Expectations: *context clues; prefixes/suffixes; word meaning; related details; paraphrase main idea; cause/effect; analyze information to make judgments; describe character; sequential order; recognize the need for rules in the home*

4. **List two things for which Abraham Lincoln was known.**

   Answer: *Lincoln was known for his honesty and for being elected President even though he grew up very poor.*

   Objectives/Expectations: *main idea/details; follow written directions; author's point of view; fact/nonfact; understanding characteristics of people in history.*

5. **Why do we study about Abraham Lincoln?**

   Answer: *He was a President of the United States. He was known for becoming President even though he was very poor growing up, and he was also known for his honesty.*

   Objectives/Expectations: *summarization; generalization; main idea/supporting details; draw conclusions; analyze information and make judgments; recognize persuasive devices*

6. What was used to cover windows instead of glass during the 1800's?

Answer: *strips of oiled paper pasted across the window opening*

Objectives/Expectations: *word meaning; context clues to determine meanings of specialized/technical terms; summarization; cause/effect; actions and outcomes; time/setting; recognize how people adapt*

7. How did Abraham Lincoln do his arithmetic when he was a boy?

Answer: *Lincoln did his arithmetic by using the back of a shovel as a slate and a burned stick of wood for a pencil. He would do his math by the light of the fire.*

Objectives/Expectations: *definition and explanation; details; sequential order; summarization; make inferences and draw conclusions; describe setting, and character; recognize how people adapt or modify the environment to meet basic needs*

8. Describe what Abraham Lincoln's home looked like when he was seven years old.

Answer: *Lincoln's home in Indiana was a log cabin. It only had three sides, and the fourth side was open to the air. It didn't have a door, any windows, or a chimney. It didn't even have a floor.*

Objectives/Expectations: *setting; time; summarization; analyze information; celebrate heritage, diversity, and culture; distinguish among past, present, and future, and describe how things change over time*

9. What happened to the book about George Washington that Lincoln borrowed to read?

Answer: *He put it between two logs of the cabin to keep it safe when he went to bed. It rained during the night and the book was soaked and ruined.*

Objectives/Expectations: *sequential order; context clues; cause/effect; make inferences and draw conclusions; recognize forms of propaganda and persuasive devices; understand rights and responsibilities; differentiate among fact, fiction, and opinion in relating historical events*

10. List two jobs Abraham Lincoln had before he became the President of the United States.

Answer: *He was a lawyer and a United States Congressman.*

Objectives/Expectations: *fact/nonfact; details; inferences and conclusions; future actions and outcomes; cause/effect; follow written directions; begin to understand the basic purpose of government and how citizen participation can affect government*

Dots'n'Boxes™

Chief Joseph—Dots'n'Boxes™ Social Studies

The story of Chief Joseph and the Nez Perce
Taken from *The Biography of a Great Indian,* Wilson-Erickson, 1936

The Nez Perce Indians originally lived in the region where Idaho, Oregon, and Washington State meet – in the Wallowa Valley area. Nez Perce means pierced nose. The most widely-known Nez Perce Indian was Chief Joseph, whose Indian name was Hin-mah-too-yah-lat-kekt. Translated, this means Thunder Rolling Down the Mountains. Chief Joseph's father, referred to by his Christian name as Joseph the Elder, was one of the first Nez Perce converts to Christianity. Joseph the Elder was an active supporter of the tribe's long-standing peace with the white man. In 1855, he helped Washington's territorial governor set up a Nez Perce reservation that stretched from Oregon into Idaho. However, in 1863, prospectors overran the Nez Perce reservation after discovering gold there, and the federal government took back almost six million acres of this land. The government restricted the tribe to a reservation in Idaho that was one-tenth the size of their prior reservation. Joseph the Elder, feeling betrayed, destroyed his Bible and American flag, and refused to move from the Nez Perce homeland or to sign the treaty that would have made the new boundaries official.

Chief Joseph, who was designated Chief upon Joseph the Elder's death in 1871, inherited this volatile situation. In 1873, a federal order had seemed likely to remove white settlers and let the Nez Perce remain, which would have calmed the situation. But the federal government reversed itself and fighting broke out between the Nez Perce and U.S. troops; the year was 1877. Joseph's warriors won several battles, but he realized they could not defeat the Army, led by General Howard. Chief Joseph ordered a retreat of the Nez Perce to Canada. He conducted the retreat so skillfully that he has been called the "Indian Napoleon." Even the U.S. Army was impressed with the 1,400-mile march. The retreat ended with Chief Joseph surrendering just miles from the Canadian border. Following is Chief Joseph's well-known 1877 speech when he surrendered in the Bear Paw Mountains.

" I am tired of fighting. Our chiefs are killed. Looking Glass is dead. Toohoolhoolzote is dead. The old men are all dead. It is the young men who say, 'Yes' or 'No.' He who led the young men (Olikut) is dead. It is cold, and we have no blankets. The little children are freezing to death. My people, some of them, have run away to the hills, and have no blankets, no food. No one knows where they are – perhaps freezing to death. I want to have time to look for my children, and see how many of them I can find. Maybe I shall find them among the dead. Hear me, my chiefs! I am tired. My heart is sick and sad. From where the sun now stands I will fight no more forever."

Questions: Chief Joseph

1. **The Nez Perce originally lived in what valley?**
    Answer: *Wallowa Valley*
    Objectives/Expectations: *details; map skills; geography*

2. **Where is this valley located?**
    Answer: *Where Idaho, Oregon and Washington meet.*

Objectives/Expectations: *explain how natural resources, resource needs, different perspectives, and trade relationships produce conflict and/or cooperation; geography, longitude/latitude*

3. Nez Perce is French and means what?

Answer: *Pierced nose.*

Objectives/Expectations: *vocabulary; culture; tradition*

4. What does Hin-mah-too-yah-lat-kekt mean?

Answer: *Thunder Rolling Down the Mountains.*

Objectives/Expectations: *vocabulary; culture; tradition*

5. Who is the most well known of the Nez Perce Indians?

Answer: *Chief Joseph.*

Objectives/Expectations: *examine how human and physical geography influence past decisions and events; feelings and emotions of characters; main idea*

6. Explain in what way Chief Joseph's father cooperated with the territorial governor of Washington.

Answer: *Joseph the Elder helped the territorial governor set up a Nez Perce reservation.*

Objectives/Expectations: *concerning geography ... identify where things (people, places, landmarks) are, how they are arranged, and why they are in particular locations; relationships*

7. Describe what event took place to cause white settlers to move onto the Indian land.

Answer: *Gold was found on the land.*

Objectives/Expectations: *evaluate past, current, and future issues of land use (preservation, development, modification) from geographic perspectives; sequential order; cause/effect*

8. What did the U.S. government do after gold was found on the land?

Answer: *The government took back 6 million acres of the Indian land. What then did Joseph the Elder do to evidence his feeling of betrayal?*

Objectives/Expectations: *examine how human and physical geography influence past decisions and events; examine essential roles of government in early cultures*

9. What did Chief Joseph do after the U.S. government took back the Indian land?

Answer: *He destroyed his Bible and American flag.*

Objectives/Expectations: *analyze conflicts on historical events and changes; explore ways in which belief systems, knowledge, and behavioral patterns define cultures and help to explain historical perspectives and events*

10. In what year did fighting break out between the Nez Perce and the government?

Answer: *In 1877.*

Objectives/Expectations: *detail to support main idea; dates, math concepts; prediction; outcome; relationships*

11. Realizing he could not win the war, what did Chief Joseph decide to do?

Answer: *He decided the tribe would retreat to Canada.*
Objectives/Expectations: *evaluate the interaction of humans with their environments; recognize the importance of physical environments – natural resources, etc.; understand the concept of scarcity; cause/effect; predict outcome*

12. **About how many miles did the tribe march?**
Answer: *About 1,400.*
Objectives/Expectations: *use the five themes of geography (location, place, regions, movement, and relationships within places); relationships; cause/effect; predict outcome; logical conclusion; feelings and emotions; charts and graphs; measurement; map skills*

13. **Where did Chief Joseph surrender?**
Answer: *The Bear Paw Mountains.*
Objectives/Expectations: *geography; culture; feelings and relationships; outcome*

14. **Quote the famous last line from Chief Joseph's speech when he surrendered.**
Answer: *"From where the sun now stands I will fight no more forever".*
Objectives/Expectations: *author's purpose; feelings and emotions; analyze how governments reflect and impact culture; relationships*

Finding Perimeter and Area—Dots'n'Boxes™ Geometry

Understanding and demonstrating geometric properties and relationships

1. There are a number of geometric shapes. Some geometric shapes are polygons; polygons are closed figures that have sides. Below are examples of polygons.

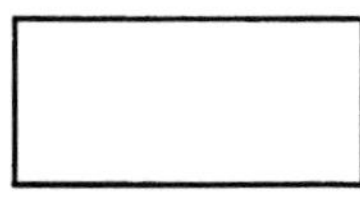
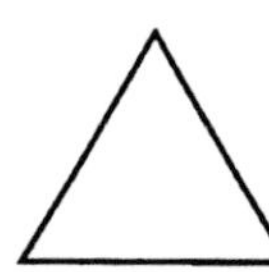
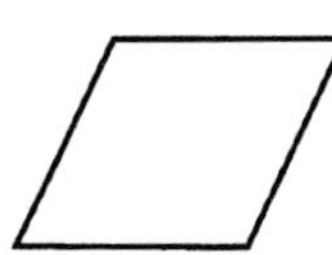
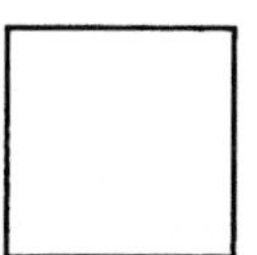

Rectangle   Triangle   Parallelogram   Square

Plane geometry deals with shapes on a flat surface. The figures above are *plane geometric figures.* There is another kind of geometry called *solid geometry. Solid geometric figures* have three dimensions - length, width and height. We will discuss *solid geometry* in another chapter.

2. There are formulas to find the perimeter (distance around all of the sides) and area (the space inside a shape). Formulas use letters to represent words – here is a list of the letters used in geometric formulas.

A = area   s = side   l = length

C = circumference b = base   r = radius

P = perimeter   d = diameter   w = width

                   h = height

Circumference, diameter and radius deal with circles.

3. **To find the perimeter of a polygon, add the length of all the sides.**
   Example: Bob has poured concrete for a kennel for his dog. He wants to know how much
   fencing to buy to enclose it. To find the perimeter of the kennel, Bob will need to
   add the length of the sides.

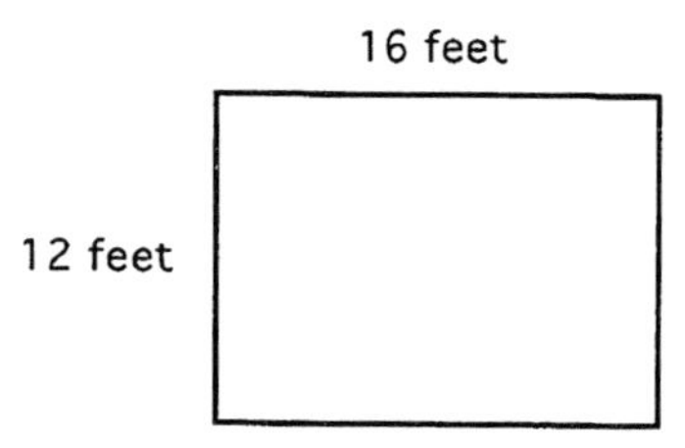

The perimeter *(P) = 16 + 16 + 12 + 12 = 56 feet*

The perimeter *(P)* of any other polygon can be
calculated in the same way.

4. **In the case of a square, since all the sides are of equal length, the perimeter can be found if you
   know the length of only 1 side.**

   The formula would be: $P = 4s$ *Perimeter = 4 x (s)*

   $P = 4 x 3$ $P = 12$

5. **In the case of a rectangle or parallelogram, you only need to know the length of 2 sides to find
   the perimeter since the opposite sides will be the same length.**

   The formula would be: $P = 2w + 2l$

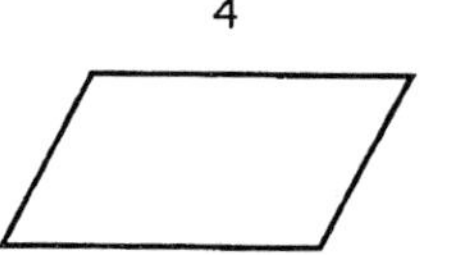

   $P = (2 x 3) + (2 x 5) = 6 + 10 = 16$

   $P = (2 x 4) + (2 x 3) = 8 + 6 = 14$

6. In the case of an equilateral triangle (all 3 sides are the same length), you only need to know the length of 1 side to find the perimeter.

The formula would be: $P = 3\,s$

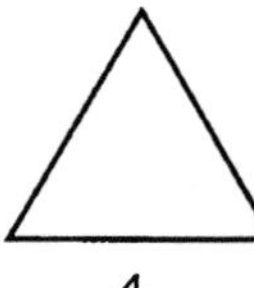

$$P = 3 \times 4 \qquad\qquad P = 12$$

7. Finding the areas of regular shapes can be done with formulas.

To find the area of a square or rectangle the formula is: *A = w x l (area = width x length)*

To find the area of a parallelogram the formula is: *A = h x l (area = height x length)*

To find the area of a triangle, the formula is: *A = ¹/₂ b x h (area = ¹/₂ base x height)*

The answer will be stated as "square inches," "square feet," etc.

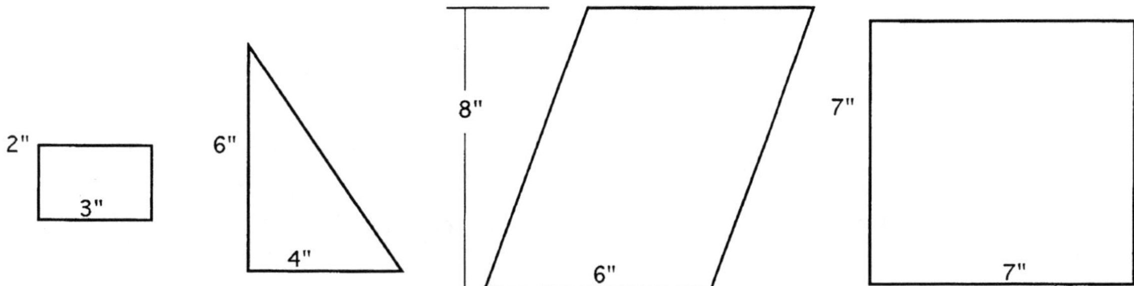

A = w x l	*A = ¹/₂ b x h*	*A = h x l*	*A = w x l*
A = 2 x 3 = 6 sq."	*A = 2 x 6 = 12 sq."*	*A = 8 x 6 = 48 sq."*	*A = 7 x 7 = 49 sq."*

Questions : Finding Perimeter and Area

1. Match the following:

A) Polygons   ______ the space inside a shape

B) Perimeter   ______ use letters to represent words

C) Area   ______ figures that have closed sides

D) Formulas   ______ distance around all of the sides

Answers: *A) closed figures that have sides*   *C) the space inside a shape*

              B) distance around all of the sides   *D) use letters to represent words*

2. True – false: 1. _____ Solid geometry deals with shapes on a flat surface.

2. _____ To find the perimeter of a polygon, add the length of all the sides.

3. _____ An equilateral triangle has sides of different lengths.

4. _____ In the case of a rectangle or parallelogram, you can calculate the
perimeter if you know the length of only 2 sides.

Answers: *1. F*   *2. T*   *3. F*   *4. T*

3. Solve the following problems:
What is the perimeter of these figures?

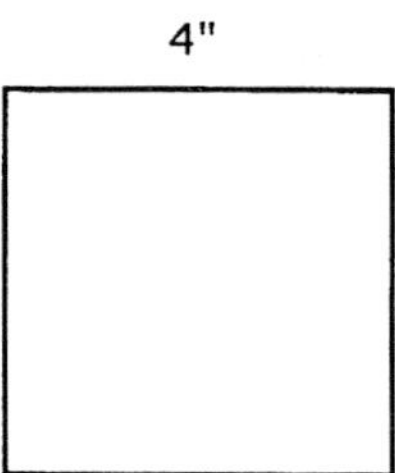

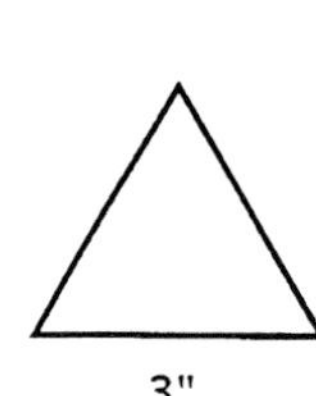

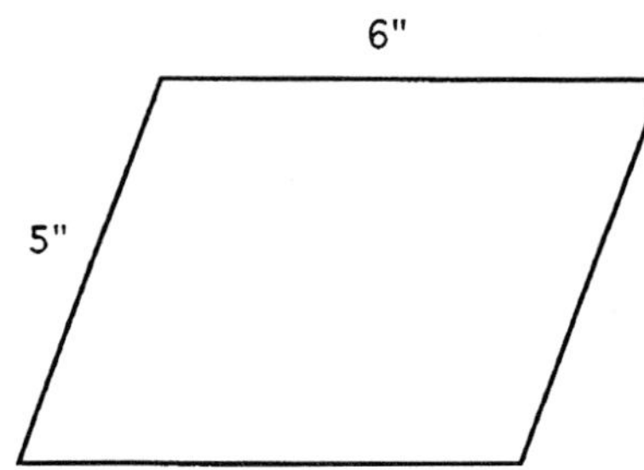

Answers:
Square = 4 x 4 = 16"   *Triangle = 3 x 3 = 9"*   *Parallelogram = (2 x 6) + (2 x 5) = 22"*

4. State the formulas for: Area of a square / rectangle _________________________________

Area of a parallelogram _________________________________

Area of a triangle _________________________________

Answers:

Area of a square / rectangle $A = w \times l$ *(area = width x length)*
Area of a parallelogram $A = h \times l$ *(area = height x length)*
Area of a triangle $A = \tfrac{1}{2} b \times h$ *(area = $\tfrac{1}{2}$ base x height)*

5. Find the area of these figures:

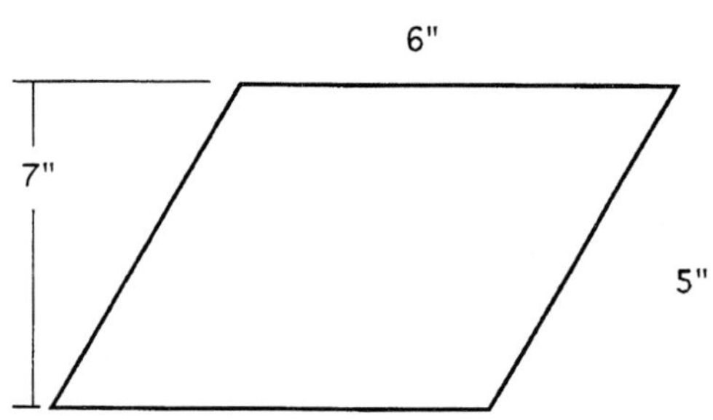

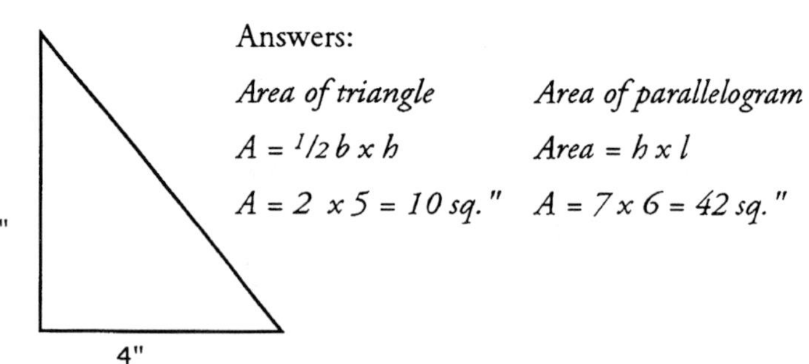

Answers:

Area of triangle	*Area of parallelogram*
$A = \tfrac{1}{2} b \times h$	*Area = $h \times l$*
A = 2 x 5 = 10 sq."	*A = 7 x 6 = 42 sq."*

Dots´n´Boxes™

Charles Lindbergh was born in Detroit, Michigan, February 4, 1902. Lindbergh is known primarily for his solo, nonstop flight across the Atlantic Ocean. From an early age he wanted to fly. He quit college after two years, and became an airplane mechanic. He then became a pilot, performing daredevil stunts at fairs.

Lindbergh joined the U.S. Army Air Service in 1924, and was stationed at Brooks and Kelly Air Fields in San Antonio, Texas. He graduated at the top of his class. After that, he became the chief pilot for the Robertson Aircraft Corporation; they hired him to fly mail between St. Louis and Chicago.

In 1919, a New York businessman named Raymond Orteig offered a $25,000 reward to the first pilot to complete a nonstop transatlantic flight. By 1926, no one had accomplished this, so Charles Lindbergh started making his plans for the flight. On May 20, 1927, Lindbergh took off from New York. He arrived 33 1/2 hours later in Paris. He had flown 3600 miles, nonstop and alone. His plane's name was the Spirit of St. Louis, and it can be seen today at the Smithsonian National Air and Space Museum in Washington, D.C. For his accomplishment Lindbergh was awarded the Medal of Honor and the Distinguished Flying Cross. He was nicknamed "Lucky Lindy" after the flight.

On May 27, 1929, Charles married Anne Morrow. She also became a pilot. They flew together often. Besides Lindbergh's famous flight, he and his wife are probably most often remembered because of the tragic kidnapping of their son, Charles, Jr., in 1932. When Charles, Jr. was 1 1/2 years old, he was taken from their home in Hopewell, New Jersey. Ten weeks later he was found dead. Bruno Hauptmann was tried and found guilty of the crime. He was later executed. This horrible event resulted in the Lindberghs moving to Europe for a period of time. The kidnapping also affected the passage of the Lindbergh Law, which made kidnapping a federal offense in many cases.

During World War II, Lindbergh flew as a test pilot, and also flew about 50 combat missions. After the war he was given the rank of brigadier general in the United States Air Force.

Charles Lindbergh died on August 26, 1974. He had devoted the later years of his life to environmental causes.

Questions: The Life of Charles Lindbergh

1. **Name two reasons both Charles Lindbergh and his wife were well known.**

   Answer: *She became a pilot like her husband and the kidnapping of their son.*

   Objectives/Expectations: *main idea and supporting details; cause/effect; relationships; situations that impacted history*

2. **Over what ocean did Charles Lindbergh make his solo nonstop flight?**

   Answer: *Atlantic*

   Objectives/Expectations: *details; geography; historical actions and inventions*

3. **Explain Lindbergh's early experience with airplanes.**

Answer: *Even when he was young, he wanted to fly. He quit college after two years to become an airplane mechanic. He finally became a pilot and flew stunts at fairs. He even joined the U.S. Army Air Service to get more experience and graduated at the top of his class.*

Objectives/Expectations: *sequential order; cause/effect; predict outcome; fact/opinion; understanding the impact individuals can make on history and technology*

4. **List three different jobs Lindbergh had pertaining to flying before his nonstop flight.**

Answer: *airline mechanic; stunt pilot; flew mail between St. Louis and Chicago for the Robertson Aircraft Corporation*

Objectives/Expectations: *following written directions; sequential order; increasing the degree of difficulty in experiments and/or actions*

5. **What prompted Lindberg to try to fly across the Atlantic? Explain what happened.**

Answer: *Raymond Orteig (a New York businessman) offered $25,000 to the first pilot to complete a nonstop transatlantic flight. Lindberg finally did this. It took him 331/2 hours to fly from New York to Paris, France, 3,600 miles, nonstop, alone.*

Objectives/Expectations: *understanding relationships; inference; cause/effect; facts and details; understanding human emotions; history-making occurrences*

6. **On what date did Lindberg begin his flight and on what date did he complete it?**

Answer: *May 20, 1927, he began and ended on May 21, 1927, because it took 33 $^1/2$ hours which took him into the next day.*

Objectives/Expectations: *math calculations; logical deduction; facts and details*

7. **Where is his plane now? What happened to him because of his flight, what was the name of the plane and what nickname was tacked on Lindbergh because of the flight?**

Answer: *The airplane, the Spirit of St Louis, is now in the Smithsonian National Air and Space Museum in Washington, D.C. Lindbergh was given the Medal of Honor and the Distinguished Flying Cross because of the flight. He was also nicknamed, "Lucky Lindy".*

Objectives/Expectations: *facts and details; relationships; human emotions and feelings; United States historical practices and awards of valor; people who are considered United States heroes; setting; culture*

8. **What is the Lindbergh Law?**

Answer: *It made kidnapping a federal offense in many cases.*

Objectives/Expectations: *definitions; vocabulary; United States law; United States Constitution privileges and limitations*

9. **Describe Lindbergh's part in World War II.**

Answer: *He flew as a test pilot, but he also flew about 50 combat missions.*

Objectives/Expectations: *facts and details; human feelings and emotions; WWII tactics*

10. **What rank was given to Lindbergh after World War II? Which is higher, his rank or Corporal?**

Answer: *He was given the rank of brigadier general. Brigadier general is a higher
rank than corporal.*

Objectives/Expectations: *facts and details; compare and contrast; military history*

11. **Did Lindbergh devote all his life to the Air Force?**

Answer: *No, he devoted the later years of his life to environmental causes*

Objectives/Expectations: *fact/nonfact; feelings and emotions; relationships; environmental issues
(specific to Lindbergh and in general)*

12. **Tell about the kidnapping of Charles Lindbergh, Jr.**

Answer: *When Charles, Jr. was only 1 1/2 years old, he was kidnapped from his home in
Hopewell, New Jersey, by Bruno Hauptmann. The baby was found dead 10 weeks later
and Bruno Hauptmann was tried, found guilty of the crime, and executed. The
Lindberghs moved to Europe for a time.*

Objectives/Expectations: *sequential order; cause and effect; United States legal issues (kidnapping
and murder); relationships; prediction; outcome*

The Muscular System—Dots'n'Boxes™ Health

1. The muscular system is what makes your body move. There are various types of muscles; some
move your inner organs and some move your skeleton. An example of muscle tissue that moves an
inner organ is your heart muscle – this muscle keeps your heart beating. Another example of muscle
tissue that moves organs is the stomach muscle – this muscle helps in food digestion.

2. Most muscles are ***skeletal muscles***. They make you move when you walk, run, sit, stand, jump, lift
something, wave to a friend, bend over, and when you talk. The skeletal muscles are attached to
your skeleton either directly or by tendons. These muscles work in pairs. The *flexor* muscles bend
joints when they contract. The *extensor* muscles straighten out joints. The skeletal muscles are *voluntary
muscles* because you can control their movement. The cells of skeletal muscles are called *fibers*
because they are long and threadlike. The fibers are *striated*, meaning they have crosswise stripes.

3. The muscles of the stomach and intestines are examples of ***smooth muscles***. Smooth muscles contract
more slowly and rhythmically than skeletal muscles. In the case of stomach and intestinal
muscles they contract to move food along for digestion. Blood vessels also have smooth muscles.
The smooth muscles in blood vessels contract to make them narrow, or relax to make them wide.
Smooth muscles cannot be controlled voluntarily, hence they are also called *involuntary muscles*.

These muscles are not striped in appearance when you examine them under a microscope like skeletal muscles are.

4. The *cardiac muscle* is the muscle tissue found only in the heart. It has striations like skeletal muscles, but it cannot be controlled voluntarily.

5. Skeletal muscles are stimulated by nerves. Smooth muscles are stimulated by a special set of nerves that belong to the *autonomic nervous system*, and by certain body chemicals called *hormones*. The autonomic nervous system regulates automatic bodily processes like digestion.

6. Any well-made machine may, in time, develop a problem. The same is true of the muscular system. The kinds of problems that can develop include *muscle tears* and *muscle strains*. Muscle tears occur when the muscle fibers are separated by sudden force – such as kicking a ball too hard. Muscle strain happens when a muscle is overused. For example, you could feel muscle strain on the first day of football practice. Muscle strain is less serious than a muscle tear.

Questions: The Muscular System

1. **Name the 3 main types of muscles.**

   Answer: *Skeletal, smooth and cardiac.*

   Objectives/Expectations: *main idea; details; examine interdependencies of organs*

2. **What does it mean when we say a muscle is a voluntary muscle?**
   Give an example of this muscle group.

   Answer: *It means we can control the movement of it. Skeletal muscles are voluntary.*

   Objectives/Expectations: *following written directions; understanding specialized terms/following written directions; investigate behavioral responses to internal changes and external stimuli*

3. **What does it mean when we say a muscle is involuntary?**
   Give an example of this muscle group.

   Answer: *We cannot control the movement of these muscles. An example of this group is the stomach muscle.*

   Objectives/Expectations: *vocabulary; context clues; analyze science as it relates to everyday life*

4. **True or false – extensor muscles bend joints when they contract.**
   Answer: *False*

   Objectives/Expectations: *context clues; determine meaning of unfamiliar words; investigate internal responses*

5. **True or false – cardiac muscle is found only in the heart.**
   Answer: *True*
   Objectives/Expectations: *details; interactions between organs*

6. **Describe how skeletal muscles and smooth muscles are stimulated.**
   Answer: *Skeletal muscles are stimulated by nerves. Smooth muscles are stimulated by special nerves in the autonomic nervous system, and by hormones.*
   Objectives/Expectations: *investigate behavioral responses to internal changes and external stimuli; examine factors that influence the interactions between organs*

7. **Which of the muscles does not have stripes or striations?**
   Answer: *Smooth muscles.*
   Objectives/Expectations: *compare and contrast; vocabulary; multi-meaning words*

8. **Name the 2 common types of problems that can develop in the muscular system.**
   Answer: *The 2 kinds of problems that can occur are muscle strains and muscle tears.*
   Objectives/Expectations: *sequential order; making judgments; behavioral responses to external stimuli*

The Oceans and Tides—Dots'n'Boxes™ Science

Tides are the rise and fall of waters that take place each day on the earth's coastlines. It is only where oceans and continents meet that tides are great enough to be noticed. That is why we think of tides only being associated with the ocean. However, the same tidal activity takes place in fresh water, but the effects are too small to be seen. When the water rolls in over the shore the water is at **high tide**. When the water recedes it is at **low tide**. High and low tides alternate about every 6 hours.

Tides are caused primarily by the gravitational pull of the moon on the earth. The moon revolves around the earth, while at the same time the earth is spinning on its axis and revolving around the sun. The relationship between the three creates either **Neap Tides** or **Spring Tides**, which we will discuss later.

The moon's gravity causes the ocean water to swell on the side of the earth facing the moon, causing high tide there. High tide also occurs on the other side of the earth, because the moon pulls the solid earth away from the water. While high tides are occurring simultaneously in 2 areas of the earth, low tides are occurring simultaneously in 2 other areas of the earth. (See Figure 1.)

Neap Tides result when the pull of the sun is at right angles to the pull of the moon. Neap Tides do not rise as high as normal tides. They occur about twice each month – when the moon is near its first and third quarters.

Spring Tides occur when the pull of the sun combines with the pull of the moon to produce tides that are higher than normal. Spring Tides occur about twice a month – near the full moon and the new moon. At Spring Tides, the moon is lined up in a straight line with the earth and sun. The moon then lies either between the earth and the sun, or on the opposite side of the earth from the sun. (See Figure 2.)

Figure 1

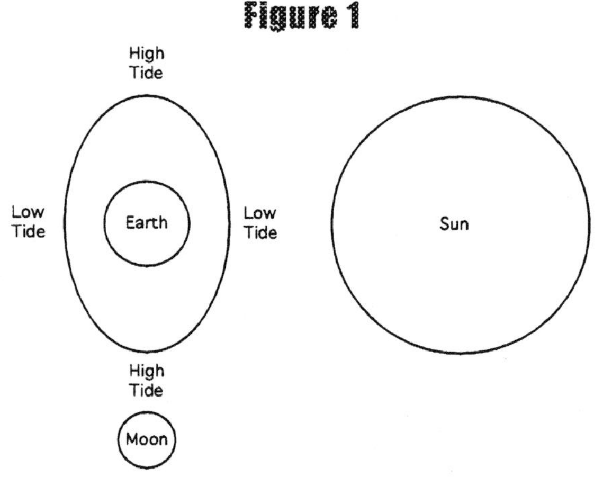

Figure 1 shows the relative position of the sun, moon, and earth when Neap Tides occur.

Figure 2

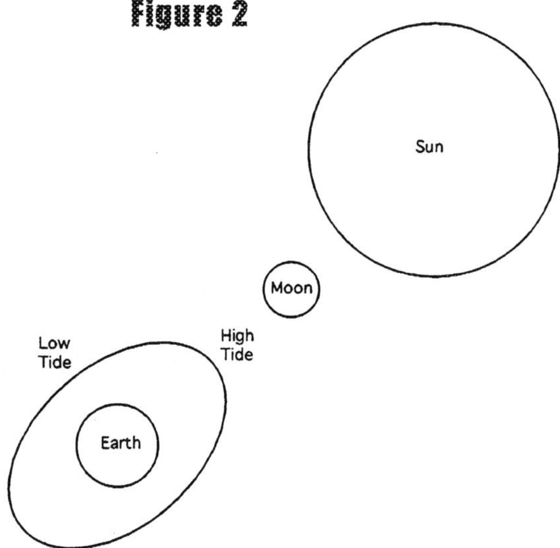

Figure 2 shows the relative position of the sun, moon, and earth when Spring Tides occur.

Questions: The Oceans and Tides

1. **Where do tides occur?**

   Answer: *Where oceans and continents meet.*

   Objectives/Expectations: *facts and details; cause/effect; examine how external sources of energy produce winds and ocean currents*

2. **How often do high and low tides occur?**

   Answer: *High and low tides alternate about every 6 hours. Consequently we know that high tides occur twice every 24 hours and low tides occur twice every 24 hours.*

   Objectives/Expectations: *compare and contrast; cause/effect; investigate forces and the effects of forces on the motion of objects; investigate gravitational and electromagnetic forces*

3. **What primarily causes tides?**

   Answer: *The gravitational pull of the moon.*

   Objectives/Expectations: *cause/effect; fact/nonfact; investigate gravitational and electromagnetic forces*

Dots'n'Boxes™

4. **Explain in more detail your answer for # 3.**

Answer: *On the side of the earth facing the moon, and on the opposite side as well, the gravitational pull causes the ocean waters to swell —thereby causing high tides. While high tides occur in these 2 areas, low tides are occurring elsewhere on the globe.*

Objectives/Expectations: *cause/effect; fact/nonfact; investigate gravitational and electromagnetic forces*

5. **Explain the difference between Neap Tides and Spring Tides.**

Answer: *Neap Tides occur when the pull of the sun is at right angles to the pull of the moon. Neap tides are not as high as normal tides. Spring Tides occur when the sun, moon, and earth are lined up, thus combining the gravitational pull of the moon and sun – producing higher tides than normal.*

Objectives/Expectations: *cause/effect; compare and contrast; predicting outcomes; drawing conclusions; understand that the sun and the moon affect the movement of the oceans*

6. **How often and when do Neap Tides occur?**

Answer: They *occur about twice a month when the moon is near its first and third quarters.*

Objectives/Expectations: *fact/nonfact; details; cause/effect; relationship*

7. **How often and when do Spring Tides occur?**

Answer: *Spring Tides also occur about twice a month, near the full moon and the new moon.*

Objectives/Expectations: *cause/effect; predicting outcome; understand gravitational pull; understand the effect of the sun and the moon on oceans and tides*

8. **Do tides occur anywhere besides the ocean?**

Answer: *Yes, tides also occur in bodies of fresh water.*

Objectives/Expectations: *fact/nonfact; explore the characteristics of the atmosphere and how the water cycle affects the atmosphere, clouds, weather, climate, land, and water*

9. **Explain the orbits of the earth, moon, and sun as described in this study.**

Answer: *The moon revolves around the earth and the earth revolves around the sun.*

Objectives/Expectations: *cause/effect; predicting outcome; understand gravitational pull; understand the effect of the sun and the moon on oceans and tides*

How to Look at a Map—Dots'n'Boxes™ Geography

The earth is shaped like a sphere. Sometimes we use a round model of the earth called a globe to see where the countries, oceans, rivers and mountains are. Sometimes we use a map to see these things. A map is a flat picture of the earth.

Learning about maps is easy. The first thing we will learn about is direction. There are 4 main directions. They are north, south, east, and west.

East is where the sun rises. You can see the sun rise early in the morning. You will be looking in the direction of east.

West is where the sun sets. You can see the sun set late in the day. Try this while the sun sets: Stand with your left arm straight out at your side. Point to where the sun sets with your left arm. You will be pointing west. When you point your left arm to the west and look straight ahead, you will be facing north. If you hold your right arm straight out at your side you will be pointing east. South will be behind you.

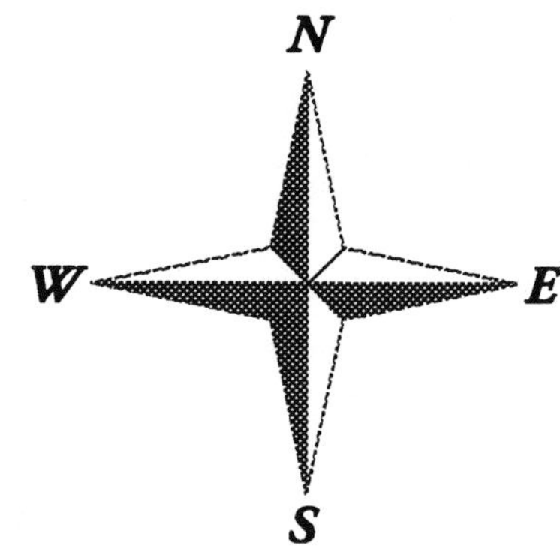

On a map west is left, east is right, north is at the top of the map, and south is at the bottom. N is for north, S is for south, E is for east, and W is for west.

Questions: How to Look at a Map

1. **What is the earth shaped like?**

   Answer: *A sphere*

   Objectives/Expectations: *details; fact/nonfact; cause/effect; model the solar system and its components*

2. **What is a flat picture of the earth called?**

   Answer: *A map.*

   Objectives/Expectations: *compare/contrast; measurements; number concepts; analyze information; review and analyze the earth's layers; examine evidence for changes in life and environmental conditions*

3. **Name the 4 main directions.**

   Answer: *north, south, east, west*

   Objectives/Expectations: *main idea; related details; fact/nonfact; investigate the structure of the Earth system, e.g., weather, climate*

4. **In which direction can you see the sun rise?**

   Answer: *east*

   Objectives/Expectations: *prediction; outcome; logical conclusion; fact/nonfact; investigate the Earth as a component of the solar system, e.g., Sun, planets, motion*

5. **In which direction can you see the sun set?**

   Answer: *west*

   Objectives/Expectations: *logical conclusion; prediction; draw conclusions; demonstrate the role science plays in everyday life*

6. **On a map, which direction is left?**

   Answer: *west*

   Objectives/Expectations: *prediction; observation; draw conclusion; analyze information and make judgments; explore the importance of scientific discoveries in world history*

7. **On a map, which direction is right?**

   Answer: *east*

   Objectives/Expectations: *logical conclusion; deduction; determine word meaning; direction; think and solve problems*

8. **On a map, which direction is at the top?**

   Answer: *north*

   Objectives/Expectations: *fact/nonfact; supporting detail; analysis; observation; identify the properties and classify line segments, rays, planes, and points*

9. **On a map, which direction is at the bottom?**

   Answer: *south*

   Objectives/Expectations: *draw conclusion; location; study of maps and charts; understand space, and dimensionality*

10. **On a map, each direction is shown by a letter and not a whole word. What are the 4 letters we see on a map that show us the directions?**

    Answer: *N, S, E, W*

    Objectives/Expectations: *supporting details; context clues; inference; following written directions; integrate knowledge; explain changes and causes in the environment*

CHAPTER 4

Heads Up!™

OR

"I Think John the Baptist and Moses Were Friends, I Think!"

Let me caution you here and now about kids, myself, and people in general. What we know and what we think we know can be two different things. Even when we say we know something, there's a fair chance we don't. Our job as facilitators of learning is to teach students to catch mistakes—their own and other students'—in a kind way. Our job, too, is to get kids to think, weigh decisions, live with and learn from consequences, and (one hopes!) get better at everything. It's better to learn from our mess-ups than to go through life with misinformation. It's like the old spinach-in-the-teeth and nobody tells you. With me, it's usually pepper, but whatever it is, it would be so much better if someone would tell you and clear everything up.

earning is no different. When we're mistaken, we need to be corrected. If we don't know, then we need to learn. This is one reason cooperative learning is so effective. With other people monitoring answers, responses, and comments, usually somebody will catch the mistakes.

Kids mess up. So do we. As a matter of fact, I don't know any of my kids who have messed up more publicly than I have. I've humiliated myself many a time by imparting my brilliance when in truth I didn't have a clue. This story is a prime example. Anyone have a toothpick?

One of my most outstanding "I don't have a clue" moments was at, of all places, a church retreat. I was in a study group when I decided to bless my newly-found friends in Christ with my matchless Biblical expertise. We happened to be studying something in the book of John, so I asked my cohorts if they realized John the Baptist was the hippie of his time: a wilderness man who dressed in furs and skins and ate fruits and nuts. One of the men in the group asked if I realized John the Apostle wrote the Book of John. "Yes! I know that," I replied.

The gentleman followed with, "We're talking about John the Apostle, not John the Baptist."

"They're the same person." I shot back. Anybody who had an inkling of knowledge about the Bible knew they were the same person!

"No," he replied. "I think there are at least three different Johns in the Bible."

Now I had to explain everything to everybody. This guy was a nice enough man, but he didn't know his scripture very well. Enunciating each syllable perfectly, I went on to explain, "I really think all of the Johns were just one person. He may have gone by several different names, but it's just one person: Jesus' cousin, John the Baptist." The gentleman who so graciously shared his wisdom every time I tried to enlighten my cohorts, would not leave the issue alone. He had on his scholarly hat. I hated embarrassing him, but when you're right, you're right.

About to clarify who begat whom, I shut my mouth just long enough for a little flicker of doubt to creep into my brain. A light came on.

Not a bright light. Sort of a 15 watt bulb. A glimmer, a faint recollection, something. Way in the back of my mind, there was something about Salomé wanting John the Baptist's head on a silver platter. Now it came back to me. I wasn't wrong . . . just a little confused—it's pretty hard to know the whole, entire Bible.

"You know, you're right," I said. "They are different. There are two Johns. John the Apostle is in the New Testament. The John I'm talking about, John the Baptist, is from the Old Testament. Sometimes I get 'em mixed up."

At that point, the leader of this "enlightening" discussion group called for a break, promptly lit a cigarette, took three quick puffs, put it out, and stuffed an entire pack of gum in her mouth. She said that she was trying to quit and hadn't had a cigarette in two weeks. I guess her nerves were a little on edge, but you'd think she would want some of this John stuff cleared up instead of letting people go around all their lives having wrong info about the Bible! Anyway, I was certainly doing *my part* to enlighten them!

As nighttime came, I crawled into my bunk, counting my lucky stars that I'd had good Sunday School Teachers and a childhood rooted in Bible study. For some reason, I started thinking about Saint John of the Old Testament. Where in the Old Testament did he do all his predictions and stuff about Jesus? Was John right in there with Ruth or Judges or Joshua or Moses? Where was the book of Moses? Crud! It hit me.

I wanted to croak. I wanted to crawl under the sheets and come out in another country. I still didn't know if there three or twenty-three Johns, but I knew one thing for sure: none of them had anything whatsoever to do with the Old Testament. Getting chicken pox by morning was too much to hope for. At any rate, I had to face the "smoke-free," basket-case leader, the know-it-all Biblical Encyclopedia, and the rest of my group the next morning.

I waited until the morning sessions had been cruising for about twenty minutes, thinking I could walk in unnoticed. That's what I tried anyway. Thank God (for real), the people in my group were a whole lot nicer and less pretentious than I. They were gracious enough to leave the Biblical Johns debate alone. They simply acknowledged my presence and never missed a beat. Everything went on like nothing had ever happened. There was one major change, though. *I* was very, very quiet. For once, I just kept my mouth closed and simply listened. There was a possibility I could learn something. I'm not saying I did. I'm just saying it could come to pass! I *did*, in fact, learn several things that had everything, yet nothing, to do with John the Baptist. My friend who was the absolute, undisputed authority on John the Apostle took pity on me. The entire group was nice, but he was especially attentive. I guess he thought I needed help. After admitting I had a lot to learn about everything, he gently leaned down, looked me straight in the eyes, put his arms around me, grinned a fairly wicked grin and asked, "Got anything else you want to confess to me, Sweetheart?"

"Well, I guess I'm a little ashamed that I've upset Mrs. Nerve-Jangles so much that she's started puffing away again. If you had started smoking, too, then I'd really be up a creek."

As he put his arms around me more solidly (you might say he took me under his wings), he smiled slyly and whispered, "Oh, I think she'll be okay. As for me . . . I have to ask for guidance every day. I'm a priest, you see, and I need all the help I can get. I suppose I can count on you when I start soliciting teachers for Vacation Bible School next year? Surely you'll be there to set our kids straight about your buddy, John the Baptist?" With a wink and a giant hug from him, I knew mistakes were okay.

I once heard Oprah say, "You can't do better unless you know better, but when you know better, you have a responsibility to do better." I hope I learned from my friend the priest (and Oprah) to do better—to learn when to listen, that I have a lot to learn, that most mistakes are not a sin, and that people are basically pretty understanding and forgiving.

Heads Up!™ teaches lessons as well. Just like me—except that I should know better by now—students think they know much more than they actually do. The beauty of Heads Up!™ is that it is so completely thorough. Students learn because information is covered through four segments, they work together, they compete, they learn how to think, and they learn how to put their thoughts into oral and written form. They learn something, and then learn how to express what they've learned. To me, these things are crucial to learning and to educating our kids.

With my "John the Baptist debacle", I knew, like many of our kids, just enough to get myself into trouble. As facilitators of learning, let's do just that: facilitate learning.

S.M.A.R.T.S.™ Heads Up!™

Heads Up!™ is a strategy that thoroughly teaches content. Learning is enhanced because the same information is covered through four segments. The students work together, learn how to think, and learn how to put their thoughts into written form as well as express them orally. It is highly competitive, stuctured, and successful because it is designed to pull students into lessons and make them active participants in the learning process.

Instructions

The teacher divides the class into groups of four to six students per team and assigns each student a role including Group Teacher, Writer, Explainer, Checker, and Helper(s). All team members are Proofers. All help with each job, selection, decision, and participation. The roles rotate on each team clockwise with each new question.

Categories for playing Heads Up!™ Include:

WHO/WHAT	WHICH/WHEN/WHERE	HOW/WHY	TEAM SCORE		
			TEAM 1	TEAM 2	TEAM 3
5	5	5			
10	10	10			
15	15	15			
20	20	20			

1. Difficulty of the question increases as the point value increases.

2. Length of game depends on number of questions.

3. One complete round of play includes four segments:
   Segment 1: Comprehension and understanding
   Segment 2: Reasoning, recall, and calculation
   Segment 3: Proofing and analysis
   Segment 4: Remediation and extension

The same theme, idea, or topic is carried through all four segments. For example, if a team selects Who/What for 10, that one question will be the focus of all four segments. The round of play lasts through all four segments until the Who/What question for 10 points is completely covered for segments 1 through 4. Until all four segments are covered, the round is not finished. Each question is covered the same way.

4. Each team in turn, the Performing Team (PT) selects a question. That team remains the PT during all four segments of a round. All other teams throughout a round are referred to as the Opposing Teams (OT).

5. A round progresses through all four segments as follows:

a. There are two parts of Segment 1. In Segment 1, Part 1, the PT answers the selected question orally while the OT writes its answers on paper for extra credit and to proof the PT. Books or reading material may not be used by anyone in Part 1 of Segment 1. Play begins with the PT selecting a question from the numbers in the categories listed above and is allowed 30 seconds to answer the question. If the answer is correct, the PT receives the point value selected.

   If the PT answers incorrectly, the teacher calls on an OT to answer the question for points and continues to call on a different OT until one of them answers correctly. If none of the teams answers the Segment 1, Part 1 question correctly, the teacher holds a "Read-Off" before progressing. Therefore, no question goes unanswered. Rules for a "Read-Off" follow the explanation of the round of play (Number 6).

   In Segment 1, Part 2, the PT is asked to spell and define a word used in the question or answer of the Part 1, Segment 1 question or answer. The OT members write their answers to receive points if the PT is incorrect. In Segment 1, Part 2, one minute is allowed prior to answering and the **spelling and definition combined is worth 4 points.** Dictionaries, texts, or the reading material may be used.

b. In Segment 2, the PT writes its answers on the chalkboard while the OT members write their answers on paper to proof the PT and for extra credit. **No points are awarded in Segment 2.** The teams have three minutes to answer the questions or follow the instructions as given. The PT must go to the board and write from memory, information pertaining to the Segment 1 question or answer, while the OT members get to use their books or reading material to find correct answers.

c. In Segment 3, the PT sits down and can say nothing more during this segment. The OT members take turns (being called on by the teacher) proofing the PT's answers. **For every correct answer, the PT is awarded 2 points.** The OT players earn points for correcting incorrect PT answers and for adding additional correct answers/information. **All answers are worth 2 points.** Segment 3 should last only about 3 to 5 minutes at the most.

d. In Segment 4, the teacher has opportunity to ask higher level questions, to expand answers, to clarify answers, to assign class or home work from information covered in Segments 1, 2, and 3, and/or use the segment as a spring board for related questions, or to lead to information the teacher wants to cover. Two points are awarded for each correct answer. The teacher may call on any team.

6. Read-Offs are held if none of the teams answers the Segment 1, Part 1 question correctly.

    a. Reading materials are closed or turned over so the answers cannot be seen. The teacher may, however, tell the students the proximity of the answer, e.g., the page, section, etc.

    b. Hands are placed on top of the material (paper or book) in view of the teacher.

    c. When the teacher says "Go," the teams may open the reading material to find the answer to the Segment 1, Part 1 question.

    d. When a team member finds the answer, he/she shows the answer to the team captain who then shows it to the remainder of the group.

    e. The team captain signals readiness that the entire team is ready to answer by raising his/her hand without speaking. Only the team captain is permitted to raise his/her hand. When the teacher calls on a team captain, the captain tells the rest of the class the location of the answer.

    f. The team captain (or any member selected by the teacher) whose team found the answer first then reads the answer.

    g. If the answer is correct, that team is awarded the points of the Segment 1, Part 1 question. If not, the teacher continues to call on teams until one team is awarded the points.

7. Points are added and checked by all teams.

8. The turn changes to another team. The PT becomes an OT and one of the OT's becomes the PT.

9. The next round of play begins and proceeds as the previous round, with the PT selecting a question and the question being carried through Segments, 1, 2, 3, and 4 to complete another round.

10. Use Heads Up!™ for any subject. It is perfect for anything from art and music to science, history, algebra, government, or any subject where information is to be completely understood and remembered. This strategy is best used for comprehensive study.

Example

HEADS UP!™ LANGUAGE ARTS

"ALL I EVER NEEDED TO KNOW, I LEARNED IN KINDERGARTEN"
by Robert Fulghum

All I really need to know about how to live and what to do and how to be I learned in kindergarten. Wisdom was not at the top of the graduate-school mountain but there in the sandpile at Sunday school. These are the things I learned:

Share everything.

Play fair. Don't hit people.

Put things back where you found them.

Clean up your own mess.

Don't take things that aren't yours.

Say you're sorry when you hurt somebody.

Wash your hands before you eat. Flush.

Warm cookies and cold milk are good for you. Live a balanced life—learn some and think some and draw and paint and sing and dance and play and work every day some.

Take a nap every afternoon.

When you go out into the world, watch out for traffic, hold hands and stick together.

Be aware of wonder. Remember the little seed in the Styrofoam cup: The roots go down and the plant goes up and nobody really knows how or why, but we are all like that.

Goldfish and hamsters and white mice and even the little seed in the Styrofoam cup—they all die. So do we.

And then remember the Dick and Jane books and the first word you learned, the biggest word of all: LOOK.

Everything you need to know is in there somewhere. The Golden Rule and love and basic sanitation. Ecology and politics and equality and sane living.

Think of what a better world it would be if we all—the whole world—had cookies and milk about 3 o'clock every afternoon and then lay down with our blankies for a nap. Or if all government had a basic policy to always put things back where they found them and to clean up their own mess.

And it is still true, no matter how old you are—when you go out into the world, it is best to hold hands and stick together.

Segment 1

Part 1: Let's say, Team 1 selected a *Who/What question for 20 points.* The Segment 1, Part 1 question could be: **"What should you do 'every day some'?"**

The team, after the 30-second wait-time is allowed to answer—**learn, think, draw, paint, sing, dance, play, and work.**

If the PT answered correctly, he/she would receive **20 points.**

If the PT answered incorrectly and one of the OT answered correctly, that OT would earn the **20 points.**

If all the OT and the PT missed the question, the class would have a "Read-Off" and the winner of the Read-Off would earn the **20 points.** Books are not allowed in Part 1, Segment 1.

Part 2: The PT gets a chance to spell and define a word(s) from the Segment 1, Part 1 question or answer. Let's say the word was "should."

The PT has 1 minute to prepare to spell and define the word "should."— "s-h-o-u-l-d." "**Should**" **means something you need to do or something you are supposed to do.**"

If the PT spells and defines the word correctly, he/she earns **4 points.**

If the PT is incorrect, the OT's answer until one of the groups performs the task correctly and is awarded **4 points.** Dictionaries, texts, and informational material may be used by all teams in Part 2.

Segment 2

Since the Segment 1 question was, "What did the story say you should do 'everyday some'?", then Segment 2 would continue with the same idea. The Segment 2 instruction might be: **List eleven other things that the story said you should do.**

On the chalk board, the PT would list (from memory) the 11 other things the author tells us to do. These include: **share everything, play fair, don't hit people, put things back where you found them, clean up your own messes, don't take things that aren't yours, say you're sorry when you hurt some-body, wash your hands before you eat, flush, take a nap every afternoon, and live a balanced life.**

While the PT is performing this task at the board without the reading material, the OT members are at their desks looking at the reading material, and writing the answers on paper to proof the PT and to earn extra points from correcting incorrect answers and adding additional correct information. The teams must have their answers completed within a 3-minute time limit. At the end of the 3 minutes, the PT must sit down and the OT's must be ready for Segment 3, which will be to proof the work done by the PT in Segment 2. **No points are awarded in Segment 2.**

Segment 3

In Segment 3, the Opposing Teams proof the Performing Team for points. The OT's earn points by correcting facts missed by the PT and by listing additional correct facts of their own. **For every correct fact the PT lists, it earns 2 points. For every fact the OT corrects, it earns 2 points.**

Segment 4

Segment 4 is used to wrap up loose ends concerning the topic at hand. The teacher can use Segment 4 to clarify misunderstandings, to extend the topic by adding "thinking" questions, to encourage higher level reasoning, and to use the information in Segments 1, 2, and 3 to write paragraphs or papers for classwork or homework. An example question might be, **"What would you describe as a balanced life?"** or **"Why is it important to live a balanced life?"** or **"Of all the things listed, which lesson learned would be the most important and why?"** For each question answered correctly, the answering team is awarded two points.

"All I Ever Needed to Know, I Learned in Kindergarten"
Heads Up!™—Language Arts, Grammar

Segment 1

Let's say the PT (performing team) selected a When/Where question for **10 points** in Segment 1, Part 1. The question could be: **When should the whole world have milk and cookies and then lay down for a nap?**

After the 30-seconds "wait-time", the PT should answer—**"about 3 o'clock every afternoon."**

If the PT answered correctly, it would receive **10 points.**

If the PT answered incorrectly and one of the OT answered correctly, that OT would earn the **10 points.**

If all the OT and the PT missed the question, the class would have a "Read-Off" and the winner would receive 10 points. If the PT is incorrect, the OT (opposing teams) get a chance to answer for the 10 points. As in the other versions of the game, if there is no correct answer, the teams will have a Read-Off and the team who answers correctly and follows the proper procedure will earn the 10 points.

In Segment 1, Part 2, the PT and the OT (as in the other versions) will spell and define a word from the Segment 1, Part 1 question or answer for 4 points. The word could be "world," "cookies," "nap," or "afternoon," etc. Again, either the PT or the OT will receive points depending on the correct answer, and teams have one minute to answer.

<h1 align="center">Segment 2</h1>

In the grammar version of *Heads Up!,*™ Segment 2 has teams working on spelling, punctuation, capitalization, parts of speech, clauses/phrases, and clear, grammatically correct sentences. The teacher may show on an overhead two sentences using the word from Segment 1, Part 2 in those sentences. The sentences may contain incorrect spelling, no punctuation, no capitalization; or anything else the teacher needs to do to facilitate the lesson. Teams may be given an assignment which includes correcting all errors, adding correct punctuation and capitalization; or identifying all parts of speech, clauses or phrases within the sentences; or identifying the subject and the predicate or verb. Teachers may assign their own specifications depending on the lesson being taught, the ability level of the class, or material covered prior to playing *Heads Up!*™

An example of Segment 2 could be using the word "afternoon." Examples:

Sentence 1: we are planing to go to the movies on wensday afternoon after school

Sentence 2: the other afternoon i say john mary and jim at the libary

According to the assignment mentioned in the preceding example , teams would have three minutes to complete the assignment in the following way:

	Subj	Verb or predicate		prep. phrase		prep. phrase		prep.phrase
Sentence 1:	We	are planning	to go	(to the movies)	(on Wednesday afternoon)	(after school).
	Pro.	verb	inf. prep. art. noun	prep. proper adj. noun	prep. noun

	adverb clause	subj. verb	prep. phrase	prep.phrase
Sentence 2:	The other afternoon,	I saw John, Mary, and Jim	(at the library).
	art. adj. noun	pron. noun noun conj. noun	prep. art. noun

<h1 align="center">Segment 3</h1>

No points are awarded in Segment 2. Points are earned during the proofing in Segment 3. For each correct answer or identification, the PT earns points. The OT's may earn points by correcting any errors made by the PT. The points possible:

Points awarded per sentence:		
	Correct capitalization, punctuation, spelling combined	3 points
	Each simple subject and verb combined	2 points
	Each phrase or clause	2 points
	Each correctly marked part of speech	1 point
	Each verbal	+ 1 point
	Total	**9 points**

Segment 4

In Segment 4, the teacher may discuss parts of speech; have the students write additional correct sentences using the spelling word as different parts of speech; or use the examples to request rationale or definitions, etc. As a rule, each question is worth 2 points, but additional points may be awarded if a written paragraph or extended assignment is required.

Estimating Sums and Differences—Heads Up!™ Math

Segment 1

Part 1: *How/Why question for* **10 points.**

How can a person estimate the total cost of items listed in the following problem? When Carmen shopped for clothes, she chose a shirt marked $11.98, a scarf marked $4.95, and socks marked $3.25. How did Carmen arrive at her estimated cost, and what is the answer?

The team, after the 30-second wait time is allowed to answer—Carmen rounded off the cost of each item to the nearest dollar. She then added the three numbers to get the estimated cost.

Shirt:	$11.98 Rounded off to $12.00	$12.00
Scarf:	$ 4.95 Rounded off to $ 5.00	5.00
Socks:	$ 3.25 Rounded off to $ 3.00	+ 3.00
	Estimated cost:	$20.00

If the PT answered correctly, he/she would receive **10 points.**

If the PT answered incorrectly and one of the OT answered correctly, that OT would earn the **10 points.**

If all the OT and the PT missed the question, the class would have a "Read-Off" and the winner of the Read-Off would earn the **10 points.** Books are not allowed in Part 1, Segment 1.

Part 2: Spell and define the term "estimate." Answer: "e-s-t-i-m-a-t-e." Estimate means to have an educated guess to round off to a number, to guess as accurately as possible.

Segment 2

No points are awarded in Segment 2.

Explain how a number is rounded off. List five numbers to be rounded off, then complete the rounding off procedure.

The team, after the 30-second wait time, is allowed to answer—**If the number ends in 5 or above, you round "up" to the nearest "ten." If the number is less than 5, you round "down" to the number shown (not changing the number). You need to know, though, if you are rounding money or other numbers (using decimals), you must follow the rounding procedure exactly as directed, carefully noting if the instruction is to round to the nearest one, tenth, hundredth, etc.** Examples:

	Number with decimal	Rounded
Round to the nearest one:	35.22	35
	46.89	47
	$57.11	$57.00
Round to the nearest tenth:	68.17	68.2
Round to the nearest hundredth:	43.458	43.46

Segment 3

Correct any errors in the estimation instructions. Award the PT 2 points for each correct answer. The PT successfully answered the question about rounding for 2 points and rounded all five numbers correctly at 2 points each for a total of 12 points.

OT's write and round additional numbers and/or write 2 estimation problems and answer them for points.

Round to the nearest one:	47.6	48
Round to the nearest tenth:	23.66	23.7
Round to the nearest hundredth:	89.984	89.98

John bought three pairs of socks for $4.22 each. What is the estimated cost of the three pairs of socks to the dollar? Why?

Each would be rounded to $4.00 apiece. Because $.22 is less than $.50, the dollar figure
would remain the same, $4.00 X 3 = $12.00

**Jane ran 2.3 miles on Monday, 4.45 miles on Tuesday, and 3.33 miles on Wednesday. Round to the
nearest miles and tenths of miles for the three-day total of miles run.**

	Number with decimal	Rounded
Monday	2.3	2.3
Tuesday	4.45	4.5
Wednesday	3.33	+ 3.3
		10.1 miles

**Award the OT's 14 points: 6 for the first three numbers rounded; 2 for the first problem and 2 for the
correct answer; and 2 for the second problem and 2 for the correct answer in problem 2 [= 14 points].**

Segment 4

In Segment 4, the teacher instructs the groups to complete additional problems; write their own problems, answer them, and explain them; or give an example of each type of estimation—addition and
subtraction—they have studied, with the correct answers and explanations of each. For each correct
answer or completion of an instruction, the team is awarded two points.

Introduction to Accounting—Heads Up!™ General Business

1. Accounting is the language of business. It is important that anyone in the business world know enough of this "language" to be conversant with its terms.

2. Accounting is defined as analyzing, classifying, recording, summarizing and interpreting business transactions in financial terms.

3. The fundamental accounting equation is this:

<u>Assets</u>	=	<u>Liabilities</u>	+	<u>Net Worth</u>
Items owned		Amounts owed		Owner's investment

The total of one side of the equation must always equal the total of the other side of the equation. If the equation is not in balance, an error has been made in the accounting process.

4. The next important concept to understand is the Chart of Accounts. This is the official list of accounts to be used in the books and financial statements of the business. There are different categories of accounts – they are:

   Assets
   Liabilities
   Net Worth (also called Capital or Equity)
   Revenue
   Expenses

5. A few of the different kinds of accounts within each category might be:

<u>Assets</u>	<u>Liabilities</u>	<u>Net Worth</u>	<u>Revenue</u>	<u>Expenses</u>
Cash	Accounts payable	Stock	Sales	Wages
Accounts receivable	Taxes payable	Paid-in capital	Interest income	Rent
Equipment	Notes payable	Earnings	Miscellaneous income	Taxes

6. In order to record a financial transaction, it is necessary to understand the concept of debits and credits. People often have a preconceived idea of what debit or credit means. Stated simply, <u>debit means left and credit means right</u>. Each kind of account has a normal balance. And, each kind of account balance is **increased** in accordance with the graphic below:

<u>Assets</u>	=	<u>Liabilities</u>	+	<u>Net Worth</u>
Debit		Credit		Credit

These are also the normal account balances of these accounts.

Revenue and Expenses come under the "umbrella" of Net Worth. This is because, at the end of the accounting cycle (usually 1 year), the Revenue and Expense accounts are netted and the resulting profit or loss goes into the Net Worth account. The graphic below shows how the balances in these accounts are **increased.**

<u>Revenue</u>   <u>Expenses</u>
Credit   Debit

These are also the normal account balances of these accounts.

7. Since Revenues and Expenses eventually become part of Net Worth, we can also express the fundamental accounting equation this way:

Assets   =   Liabilities   +   Net Worth

Owner's Investment + Revenues – Expenses

Also like this:

Assets   =   Liabilities   +   Net Worth   +   Revenue   –   Expenses

8. Accountants use "T-accounts" to simplify showing how different accounts would appear when financial transactions are posted to them. We can also use these T-accounts to recap how each account is increased or decreased; that is, by debit or credit. It is essential to understand this concept before proceeding to actual entry of financial transactions. Learn this to the point of memorization so it becomes automatic in your thinking.

Assets	=	Liabilities +	Net Worth +	Revenue –	Expense
+ –		– +	– +	– +	+ –
Debit Credit		Debit Credit	Debit Credit	Debit Credit	Debit Credit

This information can be recapped like this:

To increase an Asset Account—debit the account.
To increase a Liability Account—credit the account.
To increase Net Worth—credit the account.
To increase a Revenue Account—credit the account.
To increase an Expense Account—debit the account.

9. Remember that the accounting equation must always balance. This means that debits and credits must be equal in each financial transaction that is recorded.

10. Whether the accounting process takes place manually or on computer, all of the basic principles remain the same.

Introduction to Accounting—Heads Up!™ General Business

Segment 1

Team 1 selected a How/Why question for 25 points in Segment 1. The Segment 1, Part 1 question could be: How is the fundamental accounting equation stated, with revenue and expense accounts included in your equation? The team is allowed to answer after the 30-second wait time: Assets = Liabilities + Net Worth + Revenue - Expenses. If the PT answered correctly, it would receive 25 points. If the PT answered incorrectly and one of the OT answered correctly, that OT would earn 25 points. If all the OT and PT missed the question, the class would have a "Read-Off" and that winner would earn the 25 points. Part 1 of Segment 1 would be worth 25 points. Books are not allowed in Part 1, Segment 1.

In Part 2 of Segment 1, the PT would get a chance to spell and define a word(s) from the Segment 1, Part 1 question or answer. Let's say the word was "Liabilities". The PT would have 1 minute to prepare to spell and define the word "Liabilities." "Liabilities" means amounts owed. If the PT spells and defines the word correctly, it earns 4 points. If the PT is incorrect, the OT's answer until one of the groups performs the task correctly and is awarded 4 points. Dictionaries, texts, and informational material may be used by all teams.

Segment 2

Since the Segment 1 question was, "How is the fundamental accounting equation stated, with the revenue and expense accounts included in your equation", Segment 2 would continue with the same idea. The Segment 2 instruction might be to write the fundamental accounting equation including in your equation the revenue and expense accounts; under each account category write the word "Debit" or "Credit" to show how each kind of account would be increased [by a debit or credit]. On the chalk board, the PT would list (from memory) the equation, with the words debit or credit under each kind of account. They would write:

Assets	= Liabilities	+ Net Worth	+ Revenue	- Expenses
Debit	Credit	Credit	Credit	Debit

While the PT is performing this task at the board without the reading material, the OT are at their desks looking at the reading material, and writing the answers on paper to proof the PT and to earn extra points by correcting incorrect answers and by adding additional correct information. The teams must have their answers completed within a 3-minute time limit. At the end of the 3 minutes, the PT must sit down and the OT's must be ready for Segment 3, which will be to proof the work done by the PT in Segment 2. **No points are awarded in Segment 2.**

In Segment 3, the OT's proof the PT for points. Every correct fact the PT lists earns 2 points. The OT's earn points by correcting facts missed by the PT and by listing additional correct facts of their own.

Segment 4

Segment 4 is used to "wrap up" loose ends concerning the topic at hand. The teacher can use Segment 4 to clarify misunderstandings, to extend the topic by adding "thinking" questions, to encourage higher level reasoning, to use the information in Segments 1, 2, and 3 to write paragraphs or papers for class work or homework. An example might be to ask, "Using the correct accounting equation from Segment 1, and using T–accounts, enter the following financial transactions in the T–accounts."

(1) The Highlands Group, Inc., a landscape company, purchased new equipment for their office. They bought a copy machine for $1200, made a cash down-payment of $400, and set up a note for the balance.

(2) The Highlands Group, Inc. sold 60 trees to a commercial customer. The sales price was $6000, and the customer charged the entire amount.

(3) The Highlands Group, Inc., received cash of $8000 as payment on a customer's account.

The answer would be:

Assets	=		Liabilities +	Net Worth +		Revenue −		Expense
(1) 1200	(1) 400		(1) 800					
(2) 6000						(2) 6000		
(3) 8000	(3) 8000							

What is a Friend?—Heads Up!™ Language Arts

What is a friend? A friend helps you get up when you fall down. A friend helps you pick up your toys. A friend shares cookies, toys, and chocolate milk. A friend doesn't mean to make you cry, and says he's sorry if he does. A friend will never lie and always tells you the truth. A friend plays fairly and takes turns. A friend likes you, and is even nicer to you when you're sad.

What is a Friend?—Heads Up!™ Language Arts

Segment 1

Let's say, team 2 selected How/Why for 10 points in **Segment 1, Part 1**. The question could be: Why might a friend need to say he's sorry? The team, after the 30 second wait time, is allowed to answer, "… when he made you cry." For this, the PT would earn 10 points. The OT's would earn extra credit for writing this answer on their papers. If the PT answered incorrectly, one of the opposing teams (OT) would get the chance to answer the question. If none of the teams answers correctly, the entire class would participate in a "Read-Off". Books are not allowed in Segment 1, Part 1.

In **Segment 1, Part 2**, the PT may have to spell and define the word, "sorry". The PT has 1 minute to prepare to spell and define the word. The OT's again write their answers on notebook paper to proof the PT and to earn extra credit. The PT should answer, spelling "s-o-r-r-y" and it means to "feel bad" about something, or to "be sad", or "regret", or that he or she would "apologize". To spell and define "sorry" would earn the PT or one of the OT's 4 points. Dictionaries and other pertinent materials may be used in Segment 1, Part 2.

Segment 2

Since the Segment 1 question was "Why might a friend need to say he's sorry?", Segment 2's question could be, "What are other things a friend might do to show he's a real friend?" On the chalkboard or on an overhead, the PT would, from memory, list these things; e.g., helps when the friend falls down; helps to pick up toys; shares cookies, toys, and chocolate milk; doesn't lie to you; tells the truth; plays fairly; takes turns; likes you; and is especially nice to you when you're sad.

While the PT is trying to list these things from memory, the OT's are getting to look at the essay for the answers. They will use their written answers to proof the PT, to add to the list, or to make corrections. **No points are awarded in Segment 2.**

Segment 3

In Segment 3, the OT's proof the PT for points. For every correct fact the PT lists, it earns 2 points. For every answer that is added or corrected by an OT, that OT receives 2 points.

Segment 4

Segment 4 is used to let the teacher discuss anything that needs further clarification or emphasis. This segment is also useful to extend thinking, lead into a more detailed assignment, or to prepare for a test.

Charles Lindbergh was born in Detroit, Michigan, February 4, 1902. Lindbergh is known primarily for his solo, nonstop flight across the Atlantic Ocean. From an early age he wanted to fly. He quit college after two years, and became an airplane mechanic. He then became a pilot, performing daredevil stunts at fairs.

Lindbergh joined the U.S. Army Air Service in 1924, and was stationed at Brooks and Kelly Air Fields in San Antonio, Texas. He graduated at the top of his class. After that he became the chief pilot for the Robertson Aircraft Corporation, who hired him to fly mail between St. Louis and Chicago.

In 1919, a New York businessman named Raymond Orteig offered a $25,000 reward to the first pilot to complete a nonstop transatlantic flight. By 1926, no one had accomplished this, so Charles Lindbergh started making his plans for the flight. On May 20, 1927, Lindbergh took off from New York. He arrived 33 $1/2$ hours later in Paris. He had flown 3,600 miles, nonstop and alone. His plane's name was the Spirit of St. Louis, and it can be seen today at the Smithsonian National Air and Space Museum in Washington, D.C. For his accomplishment Lindbergh was awarded the Medal of Honor and the Distinguished Flying Cross. He was nicknamed "Lucky Lindy" after the flight.

On May 27, 1929, Charles married Anne Morrow. She also became a pilot. They flew together often. Besides Lindbergh's famous flight, he and his wife are probably most often remembered because of the tragic kidnapping of their son, Charles, Jr., in 1932. When Charles, Jr., was $1^1/2$ years old, he was taken from their home in Hopewell, New Jersey. Ten weeks later he was found dead. Bruno Hauptmann was tried and found guilty of the crime. He was later executed. This horrible event resulted in the Lindberghs' moving to Europe for a period of time. The kidnapping also affected passage of the Lindbergh Law, which made kidnapping a federal offense in many cases.

During World War II, Lindbergh flew as a test pilot, and also flew about 50 combat missions. After the war he was given the rank of brigadier general in the United States Air Force.

Charles Lindbergh died on August 26, 1974. He had devoted the later years of his life to environmental causes.

The Life of Charles Lindbergh—Heads Up!™ U.S. History

Segment 1

Team 1 selected a Who/What question for 10 points in Segment 1. The Segment 1, Part 1 question could be: **What are the details surrounding the kidnapping of the Lindbergh baby?** The team, after the 30-second wait time, is allowed to answer: Bruno Hauptmann kidnapped Charles, Jr. from the Lindberghs' home in Hopewell, N.J., when the baby was $1^1/2$ years old. Hauptmann was convicted of the crime and later executed. If the PT answered correctly, it would receive 10 points. If the

PT answered incorrectly and one of the OT answered correctly, that OT would earn the 10 points. If all the OT and PT missed the question, the class would have a "Read-Off" and the winner of the Read-Off would earn the 10 points. So, Part 1 of Segment 1 would be worth 10 points. Books are not allowed in Part 1, Segment 1.

In Part 2 of Segment 1, the PT would get a chance to spell and define a word(s) from the Segment 1, Part 1 question or answer. If the word was "kidnapping," the PT would have 1 minute to prepare to spell and define the word "kidnapping." "'Kidnapping' means to carry away by unlawful force and often with a demand for ransom." If the PT spells and defines the word correctly, it earns 4 points. If the PT is incorrect, the OT's answer until one group performs the task correctly and is awarded 4 points. Dictionaries, texts, and informational material may be used by all teams.

Segment 2

Since the Segment 1 question was, "What are the details surrounding the kidnapping of the Lindbergh baby?", Segment 2 would continue with the same idea. The segment 2 instruction might be to name 2 things that happened as a result of the kidnapping, other than what happened to Bruno Hauptmann. **They are: the Lindberghs moved to Europe, and the Lindbergh Law was passed which made kidnapping a federal offense in many cases.** While the PT is performing this task at the board without the reading material, the OT are at their desks looking at the reading material, and writing the answers on paper to proof the PT and to earn extra points from correcting incorrect answers and by adding additional correct information. *The teams must have their answers completed within a 3-minute time limit. At the end of the 3 minutes, the PT must sit down and the OT's must be ready for Segment 3, in which they proof the work done by the PT in Segment 2.* No points are awarded in Segment 2.

Segment 3

In Segment 3, the OT's proof the PT for points. For every correct fact the PT lists, it earns 2 points. The OT's earn points by correcting facts missed by the PT and by listing additional correct facts of their own.

Segment 4

Segment 4 is used to "wrap up" loose ends concerning the topic at hand. The teacher can use Segment 4 to clarify misunderstandings, to extend the topic by adding "thinking" questions, to encourage higher level reasoning, to use the information in Segments 1, 2, and 3 to write paragraphs or papers for class work or homework. **An example might be to ask, " What factors do you think influenced the Lindberghs to move to Europe after the kidnapping?"**

Chief Joseph—Heads Up!™ Social Studies

Selected Statements and Speeches of Chief Joseph

Taken from *The Biography of a Great Indian*, Wilson-Erickson, 1936

The first white men of your people who came to our country were named Lewis and Clark. They brought many things which our people had never seen. They talked straight and our people gave them a great feast as proof that their hearts were friendly. They made presents to our chiefs and our people made presents to them. We had a great many horses of which we gave them what they needed, and they gave us guns and tobacco in return. All the Nez Perce made friends with Lewis and Clark and agreed to let them pass through their country and never make war on white men. This promise the Nez Perce have never broken.

For a short time we lived quietly. But this could not last. White men had found gold in the mountains around the land of the Winding Water. They stole a great many horses from us. The white men told lies for each other. Some white men branded our young cattle so they could claim them.

Through all the years since the white man came to Wallowa we have been threatened and taunted by them and the treaty Nez Perce. They have given us no rest. I have learned that we were but few while the white men were many. We were like deer. They were like grizzly bears. We were contented to let things remain as the Great Spirit Chief made them. They were not; and would change the mountains and rivers if they did not suit them.

At last I was granted permission to come to Washington and bring my friend Yellow Bull and our interpreter with me. I am glad I came. There are some things I want to know which no one seems able to explain. I cannot understand why so many chiefs are allowed to talk so many different ways. Good words will not give my people a home where they can live in peace. I am tired of talk that comes to nothing. It makes my heart sick when I remember all the good words and all the broken promises.

I only ask of the Government to be treated as all other men are treated. When I think of our condition, my heart is heavy. I see men of my own race treated as outlaws and driven from country to country, or shot down like animals. Whenever the white man treats the Indian as they treat each other then we shall have no more wars. Then the Great Spirit Chief who rules above will smile upon this land. For this time the Indian race is waiting and praying.

Chief Joseph—Heads Up!™ Social Studies

Segment 1

The PT selected a Who/What question for 20 points in Segment 1, Part 1. The question could be: What did Lewis and Clark and the Nez Perce do to demonstrate their mutual goodwill to each other? After the 30-second wait-time, the PT should answer, " Lewis and Clark talked straight. The Nez Perce gave Lewis and Clark a great feast. They exchanged gifts. They traded horses for guns and tobacco. The Nez Perce allowed Lewis and Clark to pass through their country." If the PT is incorrect, the OT would get a chance to answer for 20 points. As in the other versions of the game, if there is no correct answer, the teams will have a Read-Off; the team who answers correctly and follows the proper procedure will earn the 20 points.

In Segment 1, Part 2, the PT and the OT will spell and define a word from the Segment 1, Part 1 question or answer, for 4 points. The word could be "Nez Perce," or "traded," or "pass through". Again, whether the PT or the OT will receive points depends on the correct answer. Teams have one minute to reply.

Segment 2

In the Social Studies version of Heads Up!™, Segment 2 has teams working on recall and understanding. **Since the Segment 1 question was, "What did Lewis and Clark and the Nez Perce do to demonstrate their mutual goodwill to each other?", Segment 2 would continue with the same idea. The Segment 2 instruction might be "According to Chief Joseph's statement, did many other white men besides Lewis and Clark demonstrate goodwill to the Nez Perce? Why or why not?"** On the chalk board the PT would list (from memory) the ways in which other white men did or did not demonstrate goodwill. The answer would be: The majority of white men did not demonstrate goodwill to the Nez Perce because: (1) Some white men found gold on Indian lands and overran the Reservation; (2) Many white men stole horses from the Indians; (3) Cattle were taken and branded as their own by white men. (4) Chief Joseph stated that many promises made by the U.S. Government to the Nez Perce were broken; (5) He further stated that all men should be treated equally under the same laws, and Indians were treated differently from white men; (6) The Indians were driven from country to country like outlaws; (7) Some Indians were shot down like animals. **While the PT is performing this task at the board without the reading material, the OT are at their desks looking at the reading material, and are writing the answers on paper to proof the PT, and are earning extra points from correcting incorrect answers and by adding additional correct information.** The teams must have their answers completed within a 3-minute time limit. After 3-minutes, the PT must sit down and the OT's must be ready for Segment 3, which will be to proof the work done by the PT in Segment 2. **No points are awarded in Segment 2.**

Segment 3

In Segment 3, the OT's proof the PT for points. **For every correct fact the PT lists, it earns 2 points. The OT's earn points by correcting facts missed by the PT and by listing additional correct facts of their own.**

Segment 4

Segment 4 is used to "wrap up" loose ends concerning the topic at hand. **The teacher can use Segment 4 to clarify misunderstandings, to extend the topic by adding "thinking" questions, to encourage higher level reasoning, to use the information in Segments 1, 2, and 3 to write paragraphs or papers for classwork or homework.** An example might be to ask, "When you read the statements and speeches of Chief Joseph, did any other events in U.S. history come to your mind? If so, what were they? What parallels do you see? What lessons can be learned?"

Heads Up!™

Tides are the rise and fall of waters that take place each day on Earth's coastlines. Only where oceans and continents meet are tides great enough to be noticed. That is why we think of tides' being associated only with the ocean. The same tidal activity does take place in fresh water, but the effects are too small to be seen. When water rolls in over the shore, the water is at **high tide.** When water recedes it is at **low tide.** High and low tides alternate about every six hours.

Tides are caused primarily by the gravitational pull of the moon on the earth. The moon revolves around the earth, while the Earth is spinning on its axis and revolving around the sun. The relationship between the three creates either **Neap Tides** or **Spring Tides,** which we will discuss later.

The moon's gravity causes ocean waters to swell on the side of the earth facing the moon, causing high tide there. High tide also occurs on the other side of the earth, because the moon pulls the solid earth away from the water. While high tides are occurring simultaneously in 2 areas of the earth, low tides are occurring simultaneously in 2 other areas of the earth (Figure 1).

Neap Tides result when the pull of the sun is at right angles to the pull of the moon. Neap Tides do not rise as high as normal tides. They occur about twice each month, when the moon is near its first and third quarters.

Spring Tides occur when the pull of the sun combines with the pull of the moon to produce higher-than-normal tides. These occur about twice a month – near the full moon and the new moon. At Spring Tides, the moon is lined up in a straight line with the earth and sun. The moon then is either between the earth and the sun, or on the opposite side of the earth, away from the sun (Figure 2).

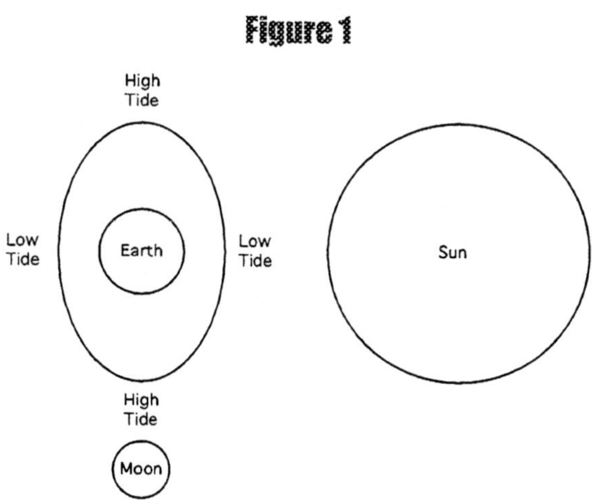

Figure 1 shows the relative position of the sun, moon, and earth when Neap Tides occur.

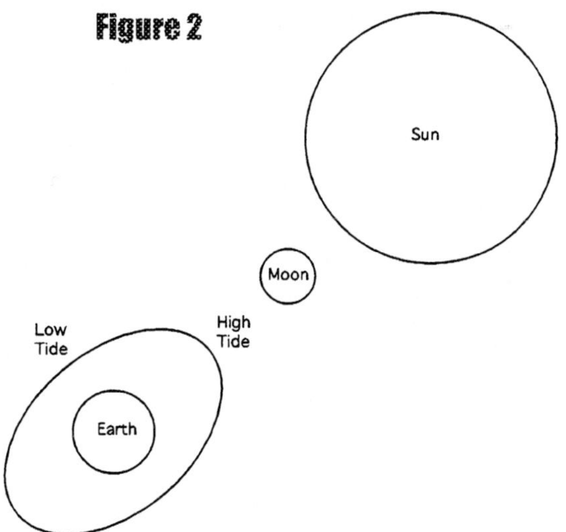

Figure 2 shows the relative position of the sun, moon, and earth when Spring Tides occur.

The Oceans and Tides – Heads Up!™ Science

Segment 1

Team 1 might select a 20-point question in the How/Why category. The question might be: Explain how Neap Tides and Spring Tides occur. The team, after a 30-second wait time, is allowed to answer: "Neap Tides result when the pull of the sun is at right angles to the pull of the moon. Neap Tides do not rise as high as normal tides. They occur about twice a month. Spring Tides occur when the sun, moon, and earth are in line, and the moon's and sun's combined gravitational pull produces higher-than-normal tides." If the PT answered correctly, it would receive 20 points. If the PT answered incorrectly and one of the OT answered correctly, that OT would earn 20 points. If all the OT and the PT missed the question, the class would have a Read-Off, and the winner of the Read-Off would earn the 20 points. Part 1 of Segment 1 would be worth only 20 points. Books are not allowed in Part 1, Segment 1.

In Part 2 of Segment 1, the PT would get a chance to spell and define a word(s) from the Segment 1, Part 1 question or answer. If the word "Neap" were chosen, the PT would have 1 minute to prepare to spell and define the word "Neap." "'Neap' is the name of the tides caused when the pull of the sun is at right angles to the pull of the moon." If the PT spells and defines the word correctly, it earns 4 points. If the PT is incorrect, the OT's answer until one of the groups performs the task correctly and is awarded 4 points. Dictionaries, texts, and informational material may be used by all teams.

Segment 2

Since the Segment 1 question was, " Explain how Neap Tides and Spring Tides occur," Segment 2 would continue with the same idea. The Segment 2 instruction might be to draw the earth, moon, and sun in the Neap Tide and Spring Tide positions, indicating where the high and low tides are. **On the chalk board, the PT would draw from memory the illustrations shown in the material they have been studying.** While the PT is performing this task at the board without the reading material, OT's are at their desks looking at the reading material, and writing the answers on paper to proof the PT and to earn extra points from correcting [incorrect] answers, and by adding additional correct information. **The teams must have their answers completed within a 3-minute time frame. At the end of the 3 minutes, the PT must sit down and the OT's must be ready for Segment 3, which will be to proof the work done by the PT in Segment 2.** No points are awarded in Segment 2.

Segment 3

In Segment 3, OT's proof the PT for points. For every correct fact the PT lists, it earns 2 points. The OT's earn points by correcting facts missed by the PT and by listing additional correct facts of their own.

Segment 4

Segment 4 is used to "wrap up" loose ends concerning the topic at hand. The teacher can use Segment 4 to clarify misunderstandings, to extend the topic by adding "thinking" questions, to encourage higher level reasoning, to use information in Segments 1, 2, and 3 to write paragraphs or papers for class work or homework. An example of a question might be,"Describe the effect that tides can have on commerce and recreation. Give specific examples of commercial activities that are impacted by the tides."

CHAPTER 5

HOW WOULD YOU ASK THAT?™

OR

"Do Tests Really Show What Kids Really Know?"

I'll bet every one of you gets confused about one thing or another. Time-changes, mileage, and checkbooks are just three on the endless list of things that strain my brain, tense my nerves, and walk me fairly close to the edge. Numerous "women from my era"—we'll call it that!—Suffer from the same malady, but the times they are a changing! This isn't wishful thinking. It's a fact. Yessirree, just like the guys, the gals are excelling in both math and science. The stigmas are gone. Alleluia! Anyone may succeed at whatever interests him or her regardless of gender, color, or culture as long as the desire, time, and opportunity are available.

We've come a long way, but we've still got a long way to go. Even though my teachers really tried, I spent most of my science and math classes sitting in the gym—which may be why my math/science prowess is zilch and why I feel so strongly about kids and instructional time. I'm a strong proponent of keeping kids in class and doing whatever is needed to teach them. It's important to note that I understood nothing that was going on in my science and math classes, and was consequently bored, mouthy, frustrated, confused, lost, and embarrassed. I talked. I cut up. Anything to keep my friends from knowing how little I knew. It was much more acceptable to me to be sent to the gym for talking. Funny thing though, I didn't learn a whole lot of science and math in the gym. Now I'd give anything if I had allowed my teachers to help me to be better than I wanted to be. I'm grateful I learned to compensate, but I'd be even more grateful if I had worked with my teachers until I understood subjects that were especially difficult for me. I remember once when I was totally dejected, one of the ones who helped me the most said, "That's okay, Lauretta. Doing things differently helps us become more creative, and creativity makes dreams come true." Looking back, she was either the best teacher I ever had or a saint. Or both.

I think the same holds true for our kids. They "get it" at different times in different ways, and whatever is being taught isn't really learned until each one really does "get it." Remembering my "glory days" of teaching, I don't think I actually prepared my kids the way I should have. I did more of what worked for me than what actually helped them learn. I think they basically memorized the test review. If the test resembled the review sheet, the test scores were pretty good. If the test included the same content as the review, but was worded and presented differently than the review, they didn't fare very well. If they heard or saw something one way in class and then saw it differently on a test, it was like they'd been given a test written in Martian. As has often happened, my students jolted me into realizing that however kids learn is the right way to teach them. Whatever helps them understand information is the best way to explain. And the best way to find out what they know is to let them express it the best way they can.

The following experience made me realize that my way wasn't always clear, beneficial, or effective. I was teaching the three branches of government and asked, "True or false: the President, alone, has veto power?" The response: "True."

Next I asked, "So, in which branch of government—the Legislative, Executive, or Judicial— do vetoes take place?" One of the kids actually said "True." I didn't scream. I wanted to, but I didn't. I simply said, "The President has veto power. The President is in the Executive Branch, so the Executive Branch would be the branch in which there is veto power." Although this was not a True-False question, the only thing my kids were paying attention to was *how* a question was being asked, not *what* the question was. They needed to *listen* to what was being asked, *think* about what was being asked, and think harder about *how* it was asked so they would know how to frame the answer. I had work to do.

When teaching a class about the Great Compromise, I realized much of what I was trying to teach was not getting through. In trying to illustrate the founding fathers' dilemma in setting up a truly representative Congress, I tried to explain that the large states wanted representation based on population, but the small states did not. As a compromise, the House of Representatives was selected according to population numbers whereas the Senate was created to have two representatives per state, regardless of the state's size or population. With compromise, both sides gave a little and the main goal was basically accomplished. Both the large states and the small states would have a say in the government because they compromised.

To clarify my point, I gave an example of compromise using students in my class. I explained that if Billy wanted to go to a concert at 5 and Johnny wanted to go at 7, but Jerry (the only one with a car) would only make one trip and take them at 6, then neither would be thrilled with the time, but both would get to see the concert. I personally thought I was pretty fantastic in that teachable moment! The next day, though, when I asked for an explanation of the Great Compromise, Shannon told me, "The guys had to go to the concert at 6. They weren't very thrilled with Jerry, but at least they compromised so they got to see the concert." I surmised I wasn't going to get Teacher of the Universe Award that year, but I will say this . . . Shannon, at least, learned what compromise meant.

We didn't have it all down, but small successes can grow to larger ones. I needed to try everything I could to encourage my kids to reason through information, so that they could *learn* to listen to what was asked and how to answer. We'd keep trying. We'd make it. I decided that from

then on, every test question would be worded several different ways. The goal was to learn what the question was asking—not what the questioning format looked like. How Would You Ask That?™ came about because I began encouraging my students to see how many different ways they could ask the same question. They talked. They listened. How Would You Ask That?™ made them talk through information and think. It's amazing what we can do when we listen, think, and talk.

S.M.A.R.T.S.—How Would You Ask That?™

S.M.A.R.T.S.—How Would You Ask That?™ is a cooperative-learning game that helps students learn different questioning and testing formats, and to process information for higher level reasoning. Students are given factual statements from information that will be used on tests. They will then decide as a cooperative group how each particular statement could be best phrased as a test question. Group work is combined and used as a test review. How Would You Ask That?™ improves critical thinking and test taking skills. The procedures in this activity improve writing skills, recall, following directions, problem solving, summarization, description, word selection, math reasoning, and identification of key words and main ideas.

Instructions

1. Divide students into groups of 4 to 6 students.

2. Provide each group with at least 7 or 8 statements/facts/informational passages that include sufficient information to allow translating into six different testing formats.

3. Each group is to translate its information into questions using the following testing formats: True-False, Fill-in-the-Blank, Multiple Choice, Matching, Essay, and Listing. Each question must include the answer, and the location of the answer if it is from text, notes, review sheet, booklet, etc.

4. Each question must be written in a different questioning format. For example, one question as a True-False, one as a Fill-in-the-Blank, one as a Matching, etc. (Note: As a rule, students write the True-False question first, the Fill-in-the-Blank question second, and then the Multiple Choice question. Frequently, they reach the listing and essay questions to find they have already used questions that would have been appropriate for those formats. Consequently, they have to rethink and rewrite their questions to enable them to follow the directions in using all the questioning formats. It's better for them to figure this out by themselves rather than have the teacher tell them to start over. In reasoning this themselves, they realize that, if they'd thought things through the first time, they would only have had to write the questions once. This works much better if students internalize their own mistakes rather than being reminded by the teacher.)

5. After the group translation is complete, teams swap papers.

6. Teams are instructed that they may copy the other teams' questions, answer location, and answers to their own paper to be used as a test review. However, they may also shorten the questions, reword them, or change the questioning format. They still may use only one questioning format per question.

7. Papers pass from group to group until all students have recorded each question and answer on their own review sheets.

8. Each group's original questions are returned to them. Students in the group discuss their assigned questions, then decide which testing format would be best for each question and answer. If they want to change any of their questions, they may. This part of the game encourages summarization because groups have to dissect material in order to make their decisions.

9. Groups then report their determinations to the rest of the class. Teams will differ in their opinions. This gives the teacher the opportunity to let each team explain which format they have decided asks the question best, and why that particular format is the easiest for them to remember.

 How Would You Ask That?™

Chapter 1: Kino is a poor pearl diver, barely supporting his wife Juana and his baby Coyotito. Early one morning, a scorpion bites Coyotito. When Kino and Juana go see the doctor in La Paz, he turns them away because they have no money. Kino and Juana leave his house angry and embarrassed.

Chapter 2: Kino and Juana return home and Kino prepares to go diving for pearls. Juana has prayed that they will find a pearl so that they can pay the doctor to treat Coyotito. Kino does find a pearl. It is huge—"the Pearl of the World." As they marvel at the pearl, they notice that the swelling is going out of Coyotito's arm.

Chapter 3: Very quickly, news of Kino's discovery is pulsing around the town, and everyone is suddenly interested in Kino. The doctor reconsiders treating Coyotito, the pearl buyers think their greedy thoughts, and the beggars think of alms. Kino sees in the pearl the salvation of his son: not only will he recover from the scorpion bite, but he will be baptized, wear fine clothes, and go to school. Then no one will be able to cheat his people again, because Coyotito will know how to read.

But Kino is uneasy, and hides the pearl. That night, someone comes to the house and tries to steal the pearl. Kino is hurt in the ensuing struggle. Juana begs him to throw the pearl back before it destroys them, but Kino is intent on improving Coyotito's future.

Chapter 4: In the morning, Kino and Juana go to the pearl buyers in La Paz. Everyone in their neighborhood accompanies them. However, the buyers offer only a meager sum for the pearl. Knowing that he is being cheated, Kino storms out of the office claiming that he will go to the capital to sell his pearl. That night, Kino is attacked again, and Juana again asks him to destroy the pearl. Again, Kino refuses.

Chapter 5: As Kino is sleeping, Juana takes the pearl and goes down to the water to throw it back. However, Kino wakes and catches her. He grabs the pearl from her, knocks her to the ground, and walks back toward the house. As Juana heads back, she notices the gleam of the pearl behind a rock. She picks it up, and only then does she notice Kino and another body lying in the path. There had been another struggle. Kino is still alive, but he has killed the other man. Deciding to leave immediately, Juana goes to the house to get Coyotito, and Kino goes to the canoe. Kino finds that the canoe has been wrecked, and then he sees that his house is going up in flames. Juana and Coyotito just barely escape and the family hides in the house of Kino's brother, Juan Tomas. They stay through the next day and then escape to the north under the cover of darkness.

Chapter 6: Kino and Juana walk by night and hide by day. While in hiding, though, Kino sees trackers and a rifleman who have been sent out after them. They leave the road for the mountains, but the trackers follow them. Finally, Kino and Juana stop for the night by a small waterfall. The family hides in a shallow cave above the falls. The trackers also camp there for the night, and Kino sneaks down the hillside to attack them. But before he can jump, Coyotito begins to cry. The rifleman raises his gun and shoots at the sound just as Kino attacks. Kino kills all three men, but it is for naught, for Coyotito has been shot dead. The mournful, bitter couple then return to La Paz and throw the pearl back into the ocean.

True-False: __ T __ F   Kino found a pearl so large, he called it "the Pearl of the World."

Answer: *True*

Objectives/Expectations: *cause/effect; inference; compare/contrast*

Fill-in-the-Blank: Kino hoped the pearl would make it possible for Coyotito to go to school and learn to ______________.

Answer: *Read*

Objectives/Expectations: *cause/effect; relationships; feelings/emotions; drawing conclusions*

Multiple-Choice: The person who wanted Kino to throw the pearl back into the sea was ____________________.

a. La Paz   b. Coyotito   c. Juana   d. Juan Tomas

Answer: *c. Juana*

Objectives/Expectations: *relationships; predict outcome; logical conclusion*

Matching:

____   1.   Kino's brother   a.   Kino and Juana
____   2.   shot and killed Coyotito   b.   the doctor
____   3.   wanted money from Kino   c.   the rifleman
____   4.   throw the pearl back into the ocean   d.   Juan Tomas

Answer: *1 - d; 2 - c; 3 - b; 4 - a*

Objectives/Expectations: *relationships; cause/effect; logical conclusions; feelings/emotions*

Listing: List at least 3 bad things that happened to Kino and his family after he found the pearl.

Answer:
a.   Kino was attacked twice.

b.   His house was burned.

c.   His canoe was wrecked.

d.   They were followed by trackers (riflemen).

e.   Coyotito was shot and killed.

Objectives/Expectations: *cause/effect; inference; drawing conclusions*

   Explain why the pearl meant so much to Kino.

Answer: *Kino thought the pearl would make everything okay for his family and his people. He thought money received for the pearl would help get Coyotito healed from the scorpion bite, make it possible for Coyotito to be baptized, wear fine clothes, and be able to go to school. He also thought that schooling would help Coyotito learn to read so no one would ever be able to cheat his people again.*

Objectives/Expectations: *relationships; feelings/emotions; cause/effect*

Prime and Composite Numbers—
Math Example: How Would You Ask That?™

Understanding the reasonableness of solution strategies, problem-solving, and analysis
Understanding mathematical relations and functions

True-False:

1. _______ A prime number is a counting number greater than 1 whose only divisors are 1 and the number itself. Examples of prime numbers are: 2, 3, 5, 11, 17, 23, and 29 because they have only 2 divisors.

2. _______ A prime number is a counting number greater than 1 and has more than 2 divisors. Examples of prime numbers are: 2, 3, 11, 15, 17, 18, 21, 24, and 25.

3. _______ A composite number is a counting number greater than 1, has more than 2 divisors, and is not a prime number. Examples of composite numbers are: 4, 6, 8, 12, 14, 15, and 18.

4. _______ The number 1 is a prime number.

Work Space:

Answers: *1. T   2. F   3. T   4. F*

Fill-in-the-Blank:

1. The number _______ is divisible by 1, 2, 3, 4, 6, and 12.

2. The number _______ is neither a prime nor composite number.

3. The number 6 is a ___________ number.

Work Space:

Answers: *1. 12   2. 1   3. composite*

Multiple-Choice: Examples of prime numbers are: _____, _____, _____, _____, _____, _____.

Possible answers: 2, 3, 7, 8, 9, 15, 17, 19, 16, 18, 19, 23, 29

Work Space:

Answers: *2, 3, 7, 17, 19, 23, 29*

Matching:

1. Composite numbers   a. are divisible by 1 and themselves.
2. The number 1   b. is a prime number.
3. The number 4   c. is a composite number.
4. Prime numbers   d. have more than 2 divisors.
5. The number 5   e. is neither a prime nor a composite number.

Work Space:

Answers: *1. d   2. e   3. c   4. a   5. b*

Essay: Write the definitions of a prime number and a composite number.

Answer: *A prime number is a number that is larger than 1 and can be divided only by 1 and itself. Prime numbers have only 2 divisors. A composite number is larger than the number 1, isn't a prime number, and has more than 2 divisors.*

     How Would You Ask That?™

Chief Joseph—How Would You Ask That?™ Social Studies

Taken from "The Biography of a Great Indian," Wilson-Erickson, 1936

The Nez Perce Indians originally lived in the region where Idaho, Oregon, and Washington State meet – in the Wallowa Valley area. Nez Perce means pierced nose. The most widely-known Nez Perce Indian was Chief Joseph, whose Indian name was Hin-mah-too-yah-lat-kekt. Translated, this means Thunder Rolling Down the Mountains. Chief Joseph's father, referred to by his Christian name as Joseph the Elder, was one of the first Nez Perce converts to Christianity. Joseph the Elder was an active supporter of the tribe's long-standing peace with the white man. In 1855, he helped Washington's territorial governor set up a Nez Perce reservation that stretched from Oregon into Idaho. However, in 1863, prospectors overran the Nez Perce reservation after discovering gold there, and the federal government took back almost six million acres of this land. The government restricted the tribe to a reservation in Idaho that was one-tenth the size of their prior reservation. Joseph the Elder, feeling betrayed, destroyed his Bible and American flag, and refused to move from the Nez Perce homeland or to sign the treaty that would have made the new boundaries official.

Chief Joseph, who was designated Chief upon Joseph the Elder's death in 1871, inherited this volatile situation. In 1873, a federal order had seemed likely to remove white settlers and let the Nez Perce remain, which would have calmed the situation. But the federal government reversed itself and fighting broke out between the Nez Perce and U.S. troops; the year was 1877. Joseph's warriors won several battles, but he realized they could not defeat the Army, led by General Howard. Chief Joseph ordered a retreat of the Nez Perce to Canada. He conducted the retreat so skillfully that he has been called the "Indian Napoleon." Even the U.S. Army was impressed with the 1,400-mile march. The retreat ended with Chief Joseph surrendering just miles from the Canadian border. Following is Chief Joseph's well-known 1877 speech when he surrendered in the Bear Paw Mountains.

" I am tired of fighting. Our chiefs are killed. Looking Glass is dead. Toohoolhoolzote is dead. The old men are all dead. It is the young men who say, 'Yes' or 'No.' He who led the young men (Olikut) is dead. It is cold, and we have no blankets. The little children are freezing to death. My people, some of them, have run away to the hills, and have no blankets, no food. No one knows where they are – perhaps freezing to death. I want to have time to look for my children, and see how many of them I can find. Maybe I shall find them among the dead. Hear me, my chiefs! I am tired. My heart is sick and sad. From where the sun now stands I will fight no more forever."

Questions: Chief Joseph

Note: No answers are included since the objective of the game is to place facts, statements, or other questions into different questioning formats. This is an example of how this may be done.

True – False   ___ T ___ F   Joseph the Elder felt betrayed by the United States government

Objectives/Expectations: *Supporting details; feelings and emotions; relationships; analyze conflicts on historical events and changes*

Fill In the Blank: Chief Joseph's Indian name means _________________________ when translated.

Objectives/Expectations: *vocabulary; culture*

Multiple Choice: The year Chief Joseph surrendered was:
(a) 1855 (b) 1871 (c) 1873 (d) 1877

Objectives/Expectations: *time and date; feelings and emotions; nationalism; Manifest Destiny*

Matching:

___ 1. Joseph the Elder	a. where the Nez Perce originally lived
___ 2. Chief Joseph	b. destination of the Nez Perce retreat
___ 3. Canada	c. helped the territorial governor set up the reservation
___ 4. Wallowa Valley	d. Indian Napolean

Objectives/Expectations: *fact/nonfact; cause/effect; terminology; setting; feelings and emotions; prediction; evaluation of the interaction of humans with their environments; recognize the importance of physical environments – natural resources, e.g., scarcity*

Listing: List 5 reasons Chief Joseph wanted to quit fighting.

Objectives/Expectations: *feelings and emotions; cause/effect; predict outcome; logical conclusion; recognize the importance of physical environments/natural resources; analyze how governments reflect and impact culture and relationships*

Essay: Explain in your own words how you think the Nez Perce felt toward the United States government, and why.

Objectives/Expectations: *relationships; logical conclusion; author's purpose; analyze how governments reflect and impact culture and relationships*

Elementary Mathematics—How Would You Ask That?™ Math

Learning to count from 0 to 10, tell how many there are:

There is 1 square.

There are 2 triangles.

There are 3 circles.

There are 4 rectangles.

There are 5 cubes.

There are 6 happy faces.

There are 7 hearts.

There are 8 suns.

There are 9 moons.

There are 10 stars.

Here are the numbers from 1 to 10, in order:

1   2   3   4   5   6   7   8   9   10

The numbers can be spelled out, too:

ONE   TWO   THREE   FOUR   FIVE

SIX   SEVEN   EIGHT   NINE   TEN

Zero (0) is a special number; it means you don't have any. If you had 1 piece of candy and you ate it, you would have 0 pieces of candy.

0   ZERO

Working with Numbers

When you count, the number that comes after another number is always 1 more. Look at the picture of the circles. If you draw 4 circles, then draw 1 more, you will have 5 circles.

4 circles   plus   one circle   equals   5 circles

When you count, the number that comes before another number is always 1 less. Look at the picture of the squares. If you draw 3 squares, then erase 1 square, you will have 2 squares.

3 squares   minus   1 square   equals   2 squares

To figure out what is 1 less, you can count backward. You count backward from 10 to 0 like this:

10   9   8   7   6   5   4   3   2   1

Signs we use when working with numbers: _______________________________

This is the plus sign   **+**
We use the plus sign when we are adding numbers. For example: 1 + 1 = 2

This is the minus sign **-**
We use the minus sign when we are subtracting numbers. For example: 2 − 1 = 1

This is the equals sign **=**
We use the equals sign to show something is "the same as." For example:

2 + 1 = 3   Two plus one equals 3. Two plus one is the same as three.

Two boxes	plus	one box	equals	three boxes.
2 boxes	plus	1 box	equals	3 boxes

Questions: Elementary Mathematics

True – False: ___T ___F A square has 4 sides, all of which are the same length.

Answer: *True*

Objectives/Expectations: *identify, describe, and make geometric figures; following written directions*

___

Fill-in-the-Blank: **Fill in the blank with the right answer. The numbers 1, 2, 3, 4, 5, 6, 7, 8, 9, and 10 can be spelled out. Give the correct spelling of each.**

Answer: *(1) one*   *(5) five*   *(8) eight*

                 (2) two   *(6) six*   *(9) nine*

                 (3) three   *(7) seven*   *(10) ten*

                 (4) four

Objectives/Expectations: *number concepts; number-ordering; numerical and written numbers*

___

Multiple Choice: 1.   What numbers are missing in this number line?

1, __, 3, 4, __, 6, 7, 8, __, 10
a.   2, 5, 8
b.   3, 5, 10
c.   2, 5, 9
d.   1, 7, 9

Answer: *c.*

Objectives/Expectations: *number-ordering; following written directions*

Matching: 1.   When you are counting, the number that   __2__ subtraction
comes after another number is always 1 more.
For example, five is one more than four.
This is called:

2.   (-) is a minus sign and is used in: __3__ equal

3.   When numbers are added or subtracted
to get answers that are the same, it is said
that the numbers are: __1__ addition

Objectives/Expectations: *number operations; specialized terms; logical conclusion;*
problem solving; prediction

Listing: List the numbers that are missing in this number line.
1, 2, __, 4, 5, 6, __, __, 9, __

Answer: *(3, 7, 8, 10)*

Objectives/Expectations: *number ordering; following written directions*

Essay: Write sentences that tell what signs are used in addition, subtraction, and
when numbers are equal.

   How Would You Ask That?™

Answer: *When you are adding you use a plus (+) sign and when you are doing subtraction, you use a minus (-) sign. When numbers are equal, you use an equals sign that looks like this (=).*

Objectives/Expectations: *following written directions; number operations; critical thinking; decision making; reasonableness*

PROTEINS—How Would You Ask That?™ Health

Proteins are chemical compounds that are an essential part of every cell. Living things require proteins to stay alive because these compounds repair cells and build new tissue. Proteins are large molecules that consist of chains of amino acids, which are also chemical compounds. There are about 20 kinds of amino acids. Our bodies use these relatively few amino acids to make thousands of different proteins. Amino acids are the building blocks of proteins. Our bodies can make 12 of the amino acids, but the other 8 are obtained from what we eat.

Most of the flesh of animals and most of the living matter in plants are proteins. Foods of high protein value include red meat, fish, poultry, dairy products and eggs. These foods also contain all the amino acids needed by the body. Many of the plant proteins are missing one or more essential amino acids. People who are vegetarians must be careful to include a variety of plant foods so they receive all the essential amino acids.

Ingested proteins are broken down in the digestive system into amino acids. The amino acids are then absorbed into the blood, and carried to all organs and tissues where they are rebuilt into new body proteins by the cells. Different cells make a different range of proteins. The genes within each cell instruct the cells which proteins to manufacture.

Questions: Proteins

True-False: ___T ___F Amino acids are made up of large chains of proteins.

Answer: *F*

Objectives/Expectations: *fact/nonfact; investigate cells, tissues, organs, and function*

Fill-in-the Blank: There are about _____ kinds of amino acids.

Answer: *20*

Objectives/Expectations: *vocabulary; fact/nonfact*

Multiple-Choice: Which of these foods is probably not a high protein food?
(a) steak   (b) fish   (c) cheese   (d) celery

Answer: *celery*

Objectives/Expectations: *classification and organization; details; prediction*

Matching: __1. Amino acids   a. meat, fish, dairy, eggs, poultry
__2. Proteins   b. instruct the cells
__3. High protein   c. there are about 20
__4. Genes   d. there are thousands

Answer: *1-c; 2-d; 3-a; 4-b*

Objectives/Expectations: *determine the meaning of unfamiliar words; examine DNA; inherited traits*

Listing: List the 2 things you have learned that proteins do for our bodies.

Answer: *1. Repair cells   2. Build new tissue*

Objectives/Expectations: *investigate the structure of cells, tissues, and organs and their functions; analyze reproduction and heredity; recognize facts and details*

Essay: Describe how the body processes ingested proteins.

Answer: *Ingested proteins are broken down into amino acids in the stomach and intestines. From there the amino acids are absorbed into the bloodstream and carried to all organs and tissues. At this point, the cells use the amino acids to produce new body proteins. Different cells make varying proteins as instructed by the genes.*

Objectives/Expectations: *investigate functions in living systems; sequential order; main idea and supporting details; examine uses for DNA knowledge; use evidence, logic, and scientific knowledge to develop scientific explanations*

Tides are the rise and fall of waters that take place each day on the earth's coastlines. It is only where oceans and continents meet that tides are great enough to be noticed. That is why we think of tides only being associated with the ocean. However, the same tidal activity takes place in fresh water, but the effects are too small to be seen. When the water rolls in over the shore the water is at **high tide**. When the water recedes it is at **low tide**. High and low tides alternate about every 6 hours.

Tides are caused primarily by the gravitational pull of the moon on the earth. The moon revolves around the earth, while at the same time the earth is spinning on its axis and revolving around the sun. The relationship between the three creates either **Neap Tides** or **Spring Tides**, which we will discuss later.

The moon's gravity causes the ocean water to swell on the side of the earth facing the moon, causing high tide there. High tide also oc-curs on the other side of the earth, because the moon pulls the solid earth away from the water. While high tides are occurring simultaneously in 2 areas of the earth, low tides are occurring simultaneously in 2 other areas of the earth. (See Figure 1.)

Neap Tides result when the pull of the sun is at right angles to the pull of the moon. Neap Tides do not rise as high as normal tides. They occur about twice each month – when the moon is near its first and third quarters.

Spring Tides occur when the pull of the sun combines with the pull of the moon to produce tides that are higher than normal. Spring Tides occur about twice a month – near the full moon and the new moon. At Spring Tides, the moon is lined up in a straight line with the earth and sun. The moon then lies either between the earth and the sun, or on the opposite side of the earth from the sun. (See Figure 2.)

Figure 1

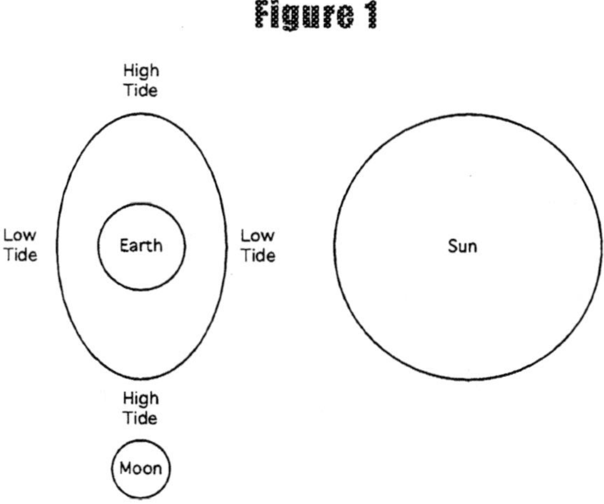

Figure 1 shows the relative position of the sun, moon, and earth when Neap Tides occur.

Figure 2

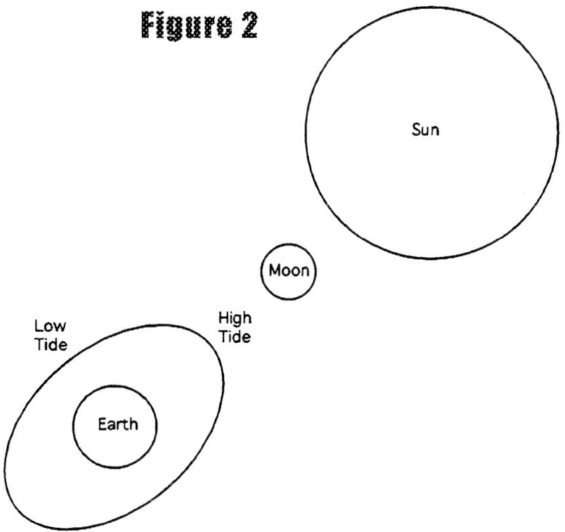

Figure 2 shows the relative position of the sun, moon, and earth when Spring Tides occur.

Questions: The Oceans and Tides

True-False: ___T ___F   Tidal activity takes place only in salt water.

Answer: *False*

Objectives/Expectations: *fact/nonfact; compare and contrast; oceans and tides; characteristics of the atmosphere and the water cycle*

Fill-in-the-Blank: Spring Tides occur when the _____, _____, and _____ are lined up.

Answer: *sun, moon, and earth*

Objectives/Expectations: *cause/effect; fact/nonfact; investigate gravitational forces*

Multiple-Choice: _______ tides result when the pull of the sun is at right angles to the pull of the moon.

(a) Spring   (b) abnormally high   (c) Neap   (d) more

Answer: *(c) Neap*

Objectives/Expectations: *cause/effect; measurement; effect of gravitational pull of the moon on the oceans and tidal activity*

Matching:

___1. High tide	a. receding water
___2. Moon	b. every 6 hours
___3. High & low tides	c. swelling water
___4. Low tide	d. primary cause of tides

Answer: *1 – c; 2 – d; 3 – b; 4 – a*

Objectives/Expectations: *main idea and supporting details; cause/effect; tidal activity; investigate gravitational forces; compare and contrast*

    How Would You Ask That?™

Listing: **List 3 facts each about Neap Tides and Spring Tides.**

Neap Tides:

1.   *Result when the pull of the sun is at right angles to the pull of the moon.*

2.   *Do not rise as high as normal tides.*

3.   *Occur about twice each month.*

Spring Tides:

1.   *Occur when the sun, moon, and earth are aligned.*

2.   *Occur about twice a month.*

3.   *Produce higher-than-normal tides.*

Objectives/Expectations: *cause/effect; compare and contrast; understand the effect of the sun and the moon on the movement in the oceans; logical deduction*

Essay: **Explain in general terms how and where tides occur.**

Answer: *The moon's gravitational pull causes water on the side of the earth facing the moon to swell, thus causing tides. This same high tide occurs on the opposite side of the earth because the moon pulls the solid earth away from the water. While high tides are occurring simultaneously in these 2 areas of the earth, low tides are occurring simultaneously in other parts of the earth. Tides occur in all bodies of water, but only the oceans are large enough for the tidal activity to be noticeable.*

Objectives/Expectations: *follow written directions; main idea and supporting details, cause/effect; understand the effect of the sun and the moon on oceans and tides*

Food Type	Number of Students Showing Preference
Hot dogs	XXXXXXXXX XXXXXXXXX XXXXXXXXX XXXXXXXXX
Hamburgers	XXXXXXXXX XXXXXXXXX
Pizza	XXXXXXXXX XXXXXXXXX XXXXXXXXX XXXXXXXXX XXXXXXXXX

Fast Food Graph

True-False:

1.   _T_   The graph in problem 1 shows the number of students who like hot dogs, hamburgers and pizza. It shows that more students liked pizza than hamburgers. You use subtraction to get the correct answer.

    Work Space:

50	pizza	You subtract 20 who liked hamburgers
- 20	hamburgers	from 50 who liked pizza
30	more people liked pizza than hamburgers	

    Objectives/Expectations: *interpret graphs; use subtraction; solve problem with basic operation*

2.   _F_   **Five more students liked pizza than hot dogs. Show your work.**

    Work Space:

50	people liked pizza best	You subtract 40 who liked hot dogs
- 40	people liked hot dogs	from 50 who liked pizza.
10	more people liked pizza than hot dogs	

    Objectives/Expectations: *interpret graphs; use subtraction; solve problem with basic operation*

3.   _T_   **You use addition to find the number of people who liked both hot dogs and hamburgers. How many people liked both hot dogs and hamburgers?**

    Work Space:

40	people liked hot dogs
+ 20	people liked hamburgers
60	people liked both

    Objectives/Expectations: *interpret graphs; use addition*

4. _____F_____ **You only use subtraction to find how many people liked pizza less than hamburgers and hot dogs together. What is the answer?**
How did you get that answer?

Work Space: 40   people liked hot dogs
           + 20   liked hamburgers
           60   people liked both hamburgers and hot dogs
          - 50   people liked pizza
           10   more liked hot dogs & hamburgers

Objectives/Expectations: *interpret graphs; use addition; use subtraction; determine solution strategies; analyze/interpret graphs*

5. _____T_____ **The word "difference" is a key word to show when subtraction should be used as an operation, just like the words "more than" or "less than."**

Work Space: Yes . . . What is the difference between those who liked hamburgers and hot dogs?
Twenty <u>more</u> people liked hot dogs <u>than</u> hamburgers.
40 hot dogs– 20 hamburgers= 20

Twenty people liked hamburgers less than they liked hot dogs.
40 hot dogs – 20 hamburgers = 20 less people liked hamburgers

Objectives/Expectations: *determine possible outcomes; determine solution strategies*

Fill-in-the-Blank:

1. If you use ___________ to put 9 hats into 3 equal groups, the answer is ________ groups.

Work Space: <u>division</u>; 9 divided by 3 = <u>3</u> groups

Objectives/Expectations: *determine possible outcomes; use division; determine solution strategies*

2. **Lindsey bought a doll for $ .87 and a ribbon for $ .32. About how much did Lindsey spend?**
Round up to the nearest tenth to get <u>$1.20</u>.

Work Space: $ .87
              + .32
              $1.19

Objectives/Expectations: *compare & order decimals; use addition; round whole numbers; estimate solutions*

3. Fill in the blank for the missing number in the number pattern:
    8, 16, 24, 32, 40, _48_ , 56.

    Objectives/Expectations: *compare & order whole numbers; determine missing elements in patterns*

Multiple-Choice:

1. Kyle and his friends, John, Donny, and Jimmy, are going to divide 16 bags of marbles. If they
    divide them equally, each boy would get 2, _4_ , 3 or 1/2 bags of marbles each.
    You would use addition, subtraction, multiplication, or division to get your answer.

    Work Space: 16 bags of marbles divided by 4 boys = 4 bags each.
                 You use division to solve the problem.

    Objectives/Expectations: *use division; determine solution strategies;
                 evaluate reasonableness*

2. The number 7 in 5,673,210 has the value of 7 hundreds, 7 thousands, <u>7 ten thousands,</u>
    7 millions.

    Work Space: ten thousands

    Objectives/Expectations: *place-value; evaluate reasonableness*

3. If Mrs. Hutchins had 23 stickers in a box and gave out 6 stickers, she would have
    15, _17_ , 25, 29 left.

    Work Space: 23 - 6 = 17

    Objectives/Expectations: *use subtraction; solve problems using basic operations*

Matching:

1. 432 divided by 4 equals _108_   a. < less than
2. 252 x 8 equals _2,016_   b. 2,016
3. 579 is _> more than_ 578   c. > more than
4. 432 is _< less than_ 569   d. 108

    Work Space: 432 ÷ 4 = 108   8
                                       x 252
                                         16
                                         40
                                         16
                                       ______
                                        2,016

    Objectives/Expectations: *use division; use multiplication; compare and order whole numbers*

   How Would You Ask That?™

1. Mona went to the park. She saw 9 types of tulips, 7 types of trees and 8 types of roses. Which number sentence shows how many more types of flowers Mona saw than types of trees?

   Work Space: a.   9 tulips + 7 trees - 8 roses =   8

   b.   9 tulips + 8 roses + 7 trees =   24

   c.   9 tulips + 8 roses - 7 trees =   10

   d.   8 roses + 7 trees - 9 tulips =   6

   Answer: *(c.) 10 types of flowers more than trees*

   Objectives/Expectations: *solve problems using basic operations; formulate solution sentences*

2. Christen had $ .30 and Jeff had $ .45. How much do they have together? Christen has a quarter and a nickel. Jeff has four dimes and 1 nickel. Are these the right amounts?

   Work Space: $ .30   Christen = $ .25 + $ .05 = **$ .30**

   + .45   Jeff = $ .10 + $ .10 + $ .10 + $ .10 + $ .05 = **$ .45**

   $ .75

   Answer: Underline correct answer: **Christen** = *Yes* No   **Jeff** = *Yes* No

   Objectives/Expectations: *use addition; problem-solve w/basic operations; analyze information;*
   evaluate reasonableness

3. Syd is older than David. Nathan is older than Syd. Vangie is older than Nathan.
   Which of the following is most reasonable?
   a. Syd is older than Nathan.
   b. Vangie is older than Syd.
   c. Nathan is younger than David.
   d. David is older than Nathan.

   Work Space: If Vangie is older than Nathan, and Nathan is older than Syd, then
   Vangie is older than Syd.

   Answer: *b*

   Objectives/Expectations: *analyze data; evaluate reasonableness; formulate strategies*
   for problem-solving

4. Sarah is 9 years old; 4 of her friends are about 9 years old, too.
    What is the estimate of their ages together - 45, 49, 40, 50?

    Work Space: 9 years x 5 girls = 45

    Answer: _45_

    Objectives/Expectations: *use addition; estimate whole numbers; formulate problem-solving strategy; evaluate reasonableness*

5. Jan went to the store to buy some candy, sodas, and cookies for her party. She had $20.00.
    The candy was $ .50 a piece and Jan bought 5 pieces. The sodas were $6.86. The cookies were
    $4.32 a dozen and she bought 2 dozen. Does Jan have enough money? If Jan has enough
    money, how much does she have left?

    Work Space:

$ .50	$ 4.32	sodas	$ 6.86	$ 20.00
x 5	x 2	candy	2.50	- 18.00
$2.50 candy	$8.64	cookies cookies	+ 8.64	$ 2.00
			$18.00	

    Answer(s):   *Yes $ 2.00*

    Objectives/Expectations: *use addition; use multiplication; use subtraction; evaluate reasonableness*

Note: Any math problem can be applied to at least several questioning formats. Most problems can
be translated into word problems. Use different methods of questioning so students know 1) what is
being asked, 2) what math concept(s) should be used to solve the problem, and 3) steps taken to solve
the question being asked.

    How Would You Ask That?™

Lessons I Forgot to Remember

by Lauretta Buchanan

When I hear certain types of music, I immediately assume the lyrics are brutal and the musician had to be on drugs to even think "that noise" could be referred to as music.

My kids hear it, think the tattooed lead singer is great, and inform me the music is a Christian Rock album and all the kids are buying it.

When I'm in the car, I keep my windows shut. After all, something might blow in my eyes or mess up my hair.

Kids want the windows open so they can wave at their friends or to some stranger sitting by himself, alone in his front yard.

When I see a homeless person, I wonder if he has really tried to get a job or would rather sit there and wait for someone like me to come through with a handout.

Kids see a homeless person and give both money and a smile because they want to.

When I pray, I ask God to keep my own family safe. Most of the time, I remember to ask Him to bless those who are less fortunate, but I don't think about them too much until I see the earthquake victims or the war orphans on the nightly news.

My kids say, "Mom, let's send some of our clothes and food to those people in Bosnia." They give half their rooms to Toys for Tots and their lunch money to Save the Children.

I miss birthdays and send gifts overnight delivery because I'm so busy. Sometimes I send a check or cash and convince myself I'm being thoughtful to let the kids pick out what they want.

My kids listen all year long to hear us say, "Wouldn't it be great to have one of those." or "Boy, that would certainly come in handy." They plot, plan, save, shop, and compare brands to make sure Mom and Dad get the very, very best.

When I look at kids, I have to wonder, "How'd they become this generous, thoughtful, and kind?" I could learn a lot from them if I'd just open my eyes, ears, heart... and remember!

™
S.M.A.R.T.S.
Self-Motivational and Recreational
Teaching Strategies

BIBLIOGRAPHY

Jantzen, P. Michael. *Life Science*. New York: Macmillan Publishing Company, 1986.

The World Book Encyclopedia, 1980.

Hirsch, E. *What Your 1ˢᵗ Grader Needs to Know*. New York: Dell Publishing, 1991.

Fee, Chester Anders. *Chief Joseph: The Biography of a Great Indian*. New York: Wilson-Erickson International, 1936.

Hirsch, E. *What Your 5ᵗʰ Grader Needs to Know*. New York; Dell Publishing, 1993.

Moredock, Janet. *Handy Homework Helper—Math*. Lincolnwood, IL. Publications International, Ltd., 1998.

Kaplan, Jerome. *TEK-Based TAAS Coach Mathematics Grade 5*. New York: Educational Design, 2000.

Raatma, Lucia. *Safety on the School Bus*. Minnesota: Capstone Press, 1999.

National School Transportation Association. *http://www.schooltrans.com*.

Davis, Lucile. *Charles Lindbergh*. Minnesota: Capstone Press, 1999.

American Medical Association. *Encyclopedia of Medicine*. New York: Random House, 1989.

Densman, Grant, Hirschfeld, Mungenast and Ross. *Human Biology and Health*. New Jersey: Prentice Hall, 1994.

McQuaig, Douglas. *College Accounting*. Boston: Houghton Mifflin, 1994.

Merki, Mary and Merki, Don. *Health*. California: Glencoe Publishing Company, 1987.

Steinbeck, John. *The Pearl*. New York: Viking Press, 1947.

S.M.A.R.T.S.
Self-Motivational and Recreational
Teaching Strategies
TM

☐ I would like to schedule a S.M.A.R.T.S.™ Seminar. Please contact me.

☐ Add me to your mailing list to receive information on new products, updates, and other information including upcoming seminars in my area.

I would like to purchase

☐ Teaching the S.M.A.R.T.S.™ Way Book 1   qty _______ x $18.00 = _________
☐ Teaching the S.M.A.R.T.S.™ Way Book 2   qty _______ x $18.00 = _________
☐ S.M.A.R.T.S.™ Intelligence Team T-shirt   qty _______ x $16.50 = _________
☐ S.M.A.R.T.S.™ Cap   qty _______ x $16.50 = _________
☐ "To Be Remembered" Bookmark (each)   qty _______ x $2.00 = _________
☐ "To Be Remembered" Bookmarks (10)   qty _______ x $15.00 = _________

Shipping and handling is included in prices.

Subtotal: _________ *

Texas residents add 8.25% sales tax _________

Inquiries about quantity discounts may be sent to us via our fax number or web site.   **Total:** _________

* *If tax exempt and in Texas, please fax your exemption or resale certificate to 254-776-3136 so we can process your order. We have blank certificates available; call, fax or e-mail us via the website to get one.*

Name ____

Street Address ___________________________________

City, State, Zip __________________________________

Phone No. (___ *)* _______________________________

e-mail ____

I attended a S.M.A.R.T.S.™ Workshop/Seminar in

_____________________________ *(city/state) on* ________________ *(date).*

The Trainer was _____________________   **Please help us by supplying this information.**

Payment Method: ☐ *Check enclosed (please include the following information on your check:*
DL number and state
Home address
Home phone and work phone

☐ *Credit Card*
Visa or Mastercard (please circle) Card No. _______________________
Expiration Date, month and year _______________________________

MAIL TO: S.M.A.R.T.S.™ Learning System
P.O. Box 7930
Waco. TX 76714-7930

Visit our website, **www.smartslearningsystem.com,** to contact us via e-mail.

Phone: 254-776-6664   Fax: 254-776-3136

S.M.A.R.T.S.™ Learning System, P.O. Box 7930, Waco. TX 76714-7930
Visit our website or contact us via e-mail at **www.smartslearningsystem.com**
Phone: 254-776-6664 • Fax: 254-776-3136